Passionate Renewal:
Jewish Poetry in Britain since 1945 – an anthology

edited by
Peter Lawson

LEICESTER CITY LIBRARIES

X84039798X-1 - 243	
	18/4/05
821	£14.99

Five Leaves
www.fiveleaves.co.uk

in association with the
European Jewish Publication Society

ejps

Passionate Renewal
Published in 2001 by Five Leaves Publications,
PO Box 81, Nottingham NG5 4ER, Britain
www.fiveleaves.co.uk

Five Leaves acknowledge financial support from

ISBN 0 907123 73 2
Typeset by 4 Sheets Design and Print Limited
Printed in Great Britain by Technical Print Services

Copyright:
collection copyright
Five Leaves Publications 2001.

Extracts from *The Manager* by Richard Burns are by permission
of Bellew Publishing Ltd; Elaine Feinstein's poems are printed
by permission of Carcanet Press Ltd; Karen Gershon's poems
appear courtesy of her literary executors; Michael Hamburger's
poems are printed by permission of Anvil Press Ltd; A.C. Jacobs'
poems are printed by permission of The Menard Press/Hearing
Eye; Joanne Limburg's poems are printed by permission of
Bloodaxe Books Ltd; Jon Silkin's poems appear courtesy of the
Trustees of his Literary Estate. In all other cases copyright rests
with the individual contributors.

No part of this work may be reproduced, stored in retrieval
systems, or transmitted in any form, or by any means, electronic,
mechanical, photocopying or otherwise, without prior permission
of the copyright holders.

Passionate Renewal is published in association with the
European Jewish Publication Society, a registered charity which
gives grants to assist in the publication and distribution of books
relevant to Jewish literature, history, religion, philosophy,
politics and culture. EJPS, PO Box 19948, London N3 3XJ.
Website: www.ejps.org.uk

Contents

Elaine Feinstein

Introduction

To ask "What is Jewish Poetry?" is to guarantee conflicting, multiple answers. Are we looking here for Jewish religious poetry? If so, we are likely to be disappointed. Only a few of the poems included in this anthology bear directly on Judaism. Perhaps we expect to find no thematic differences between poetry by Jews and Gentiles of post-War Britain? Such a suggestion, again, is refutable by myriad examples. Certain thematic concerns do recur in poetry written by British Jews.

Some of us may find the very notion of Jewish poetry in English puzzling. Linguistic essentialists might argue that poetry can only be Jewish if it is written in a Jewish language, such as "Yiddish, Hebrew, and Ladino."[1] Jewish poets in Britain, however, use English as their first language.

Others may readily accept the existence of a non-religious, Anglophone Jewish poetry because they define Jewish literature biologically, as being written by those born of Jewish parents. Again, this approach is reductive, and undervalues the importance of the specific contexts in which British Jewish poets write. In short, it prioritises the concept of race over environment.

Without dismissing the debate about whether Jewishness constitutes a religious, linguistic or racial identity, I am editorially inclined to a more environmental perspective. Consequently, *Passionate Renewal* presents Jewish poets in Britain as members of a minority group, who write as Jews because of specific social, cultural and historical experiences.

Interestingly, the question of "who is a Jew?" is by no means settled among British Jewish poets. Two British Jews refused to participate in this anthology because they did not wish to be labelled as "Jewish" poets. Rather than feeling like members of a minority group in Britain, these poets consider themselves British individuals who prefer not to be ghettoised. One poet wrote that she did not "fit into" the anthology; that she was "not a Jewish poet, but an English poet with Jewish forebears."

Passionate Renewal is not, however, an argument for some sort of particularist, hermetic literature impermeable to other influences and inspirations. It aims simply to illustrate poetic traditions and practices in which British Jewish poets are not marginalised. British Jews have contributed enormously to British poetry since the Second World War; just as they have to (polyglot) Jewish poetry.

Although this anthology starts at 1945, after the Holocaust, British Jewish poetry has a longer history. No genealogy would be complete without mention, in particular, of the First World War poets Isaac Rosenberg and Siegfried Sassoon. Rosenberg (1890-1918) was the first avowedly Anglo-Jewish poet of the twentieth century to reach a wide British readership. His 'Break of Day in the Trenches' has been described by Paul Fussell as "the greatest poem of the war."[2] Other poems, such as 'Chagrin' and the verse-play *Moses*, are also essential reading if one is to understand British Jewish poetry's roots.

By contrast, Siegfried Sassoon (1886-1967) related to his Jewishness less positively than Rosenberg. Rather than seek a British Jewish identity in the present and future, he located Jewishness in the past (the biblical Israel of the Old Testament) and an orientalised East (where his paternal Iraqi Jewish ancestors had lived). Read in this context, poems such as 'Ancestors' and 'Ancient History' offer fascinating insights into Sassoon's Anglo-Jewish self-image.

Then there are the inter-War poets, such as Lazarus Aaronson, A. Abrahams, Gilbert Frankau, Louis Golding, Joseph Leftwich, Julius Lipton, John Rodker, James Singer and Humbert Wolfe. They, too, merit reading and research as part of British Jewry's poetic heritage.

2

Finally, there is the short history of Yiddish poetry in Britain. The Lithuanian-Jewish poet Anna Margolin visited London as a young woman, before settling in New York in 1914. Itzak Manger moved to London from Bukovina, having fled the Nazis, and emigrated to New York in 1951. Most famously, A.N. Stencl quit Poland for London in 1934, where he remained in "Whitechapel, *Shtetl* of Britain" (the title he gave to a volume of poems published in 1961) for the rest of his life. Stencl also edited the Yiddish literary journal *Loshn un Lebn* (*Language and Life*). Joseph Leftwich translated Stencl, among many other poets, and was himself a Yiddish poet and anthologist of Jewish literature in, for example, *The Jewish Omnibus* (1933) and *The Golden Peacock: An Anthology of Yiddish Poetry* (1939).

Only one woman, Anna Margolin, features in the above selection of poets from the first part of the twentieth century. By contrast, six of the twenty poets represented in *Passionate Renewal* are women. Alas, there has not been space to include other impressive poets, such as Wanda Barford, Nadine Brummer, Lynette Craig, Sue Hubbard, Shirley Toulson and Michelene Wandor. As these names suggest, poetic expression by Jewish women has burgeoned since 1945.

Regarding male poets, A. Alvarez, Anthony Barnett, Harry Fainlight, Chaim Lewis, Harold Pinter and Anthony Rudolf are similarly not included here, also for reasons of space.

(2)

Historical, social and cultural experiences locate British Jews in specific contexts. For example, when Ruth Fainlight considers a meteor hurtling through space in 'The Fall', and Elaine Feinstein writes on global communication in 'Some Thoughts on Where', both poets are reflecting on universals. However, Fainlight's poem is also a reflection on a homelessness traditionally associated with the ancient archetype of the Wandering Jew, as well as her own journeying between countries

3

(America, where she was born; and Britain, where she has lived since 1946). "Wherever your home was, having left it/There can be no other," she writes: "you will not find/A resting place – nor end your journeying." On a more upbeat note, Feinstein conveys exhilaration as she contemplates the "mythic/nomad." Her wandering Jew is "lovely Allen" (Ginsberg), who is "beamed to us" by satellite. Ginsberg is depicted as following the biblical injunction for Jews to be a light ("beamed") unto the nations. Feinstein's positive take on the American-Jewish poet emphasises his universality: he is at home on "telly," "telstar," and in "the world." This is contrasted with Feinstein's own sense of belonging in England: "our local bother of where/we belong." Here, "bother" also suggests a certain restlessness and unease about this English home.

Similarly, Michael Hamburger is uneasily at home in England. The poem 'Homeless' comments by thematic association on Hamburger's series of *Tree Poems*, set in Suffolk. Far from the pastoral, nurturing observation of *Tree Poems*, 'Homeless' presents a suddenly strange landscape, with a (dis-eased) growth upon it: "In the garden grown mountainous, rocky/Some blight had settled on the trunk of a tree." Closer examination of the tree reveals: "a human body,/Not a corpse afloat." The body is passively "immersed" in "a pool" of water ("suspended" like the carp in Hamburger's earlier poem 'Woodland Lake'). Juxtaposed with this corpse-like life of suspension above the land are the animals who roam, confidently at home: "Other animals walked or loitered/As though they had always lived there." Unexpectedly, the narrator is trapped by hostile deer who "Barred my way, took over." No longer the controlling gardener, comfortable with nature, Hamburger's persona meets Others who threaten his habitual sense of a benign, English pastoral. Here the stereotype of Jewish unease with nature is imaginatively reconstructed by means of powerful, resonating symbols (as in a dream. 'Homeless' is one of Hamburger's *Dream Poems*).

4

Significantly, Hamburger is one of the seven poets in this anthology who were not born in Britain (the others are Ruth Fainlight, Karen Gershon, Michael Horovitz, Lotte Kramer, Gerda Mayer and George Szirtes). He is also one of five poets who emigrated to this country to escape Nazism in the 1930s (along with Horovitz, Gershon, Kramer and Mayer). I have included such foreign-born poets on the grounds that they all arrived in Britain as children or adolescents (Kramer aged sixteen, Fainlight and Gershon fifteen, Mayer eleven, Hamburger nine, Szirtes eight, and Horovitz just two). More pertinently, all chose as adults to write in English.

(3)

Inevitably, the Holocaust figures in this anthology. Three of the poets included here (Gershon, Kramer and Mayer) were sent from continental Europe on a *kindertransport* (children's transport) to Britain, just before flight from Hitler became impossible. Gershon writes about leaving Germany for England in 'The Children's Exodus': "At Dovercourt the winter sea/was like God's mercy vast and wild." Kramer recalls spotting England's "lighthouse of love" when she crossed the Channel ('At Dover Harbour'). Mayer pens a letter to the father she never saw again after 1939 ('Make Believe'). Naturally, all three poets write on other subjects as well: from Jewish family ritual (Kramer's 'The Tablecloth') to English antisemitism (Mayer's 'Toad').

Dannie Abse speaks for many secular British Jews when he confesses: "Dear love, Auschwitz made me/more of a Jew than Moses did" ('White Balloon'). Abse's 'A Night Out' is rightly one of the most anthologised of Holocaust poems, and is included here. I have also included Shoah-related poems by Philip Hobsbaum, ('Professor Grottmann Explains Everything'), Emanuel Litvinoff ('Poem for an Heretical Avenger') and Bernard Kops ('For the Record'), among others.

The focus of this anthology, though, remains the specific experiences of being a British Jew. As Anthony Rudolf writes in an earlier (international) anthology of Jewish poetry, *Voices Within The Ark* (1980): "There are structures of shared feeling and common perception bequeathed by a dynamic heritage; there are psychic tensions created and psychic energies released (blocked too in certain quarters) by the dialectical components of that heritage."[3] It is an illustration of this dynamism, since the Second World War, which *Passionate Renewal* offers the reader.

Jon Silkin expresses effectively the situation described by Rudolf in 'The Jews in England'. This work is structured as a dialogue between a "tender gentile woman" and a male Jew who has "brought us this,/a poem that is a single note, of praise, the psalms/fresh as a changing glance, a fragrant look,/in an English we had not, but on our tongues/makes our lives new." Silkin emphasises the contribution the Old Testament and its rhythms have made to English through translation. He locates Jewishness in the English language, and therefore in English literature. Indeed, with his characteristically robust idealism, Silkin offers a merging of Jewishness and Englishness through the image of "a thresher,/where wheat, stalk, haulm, and staff of floury seeds/like torches, stand, each eye broaching the same vision."

At the centre of Silkin's vision is what he describes in 'The ship's pasture' as "a local habitation." Silkin lived most of his adult life around Leeds and Newcastle, and it was in a "local" (as, crucially, distinguished from parochial) northern space that he found his peace of mind:

> Northwards,
> a new Jerusalem with the lamb lies separate,
> its shade dense and lovely. The woman
> starts again, as though each portion of this
> were knit afresh.

Here "Jerusalem" is located in the north with "the lamb" of Isaiah 11:6-8. In many English Bibles, Isaiah's Old Testament vision is complacently glossed as "Christ's peaceable kingdom." As Silkin remarked in interview with me: "Why could not one have Isaiah as a recognition mark for the Jews? Although I think I can tell you why: because the Church has collared Isaiah for itself. It claims it prophesied the coming of Christ."[4] That said, Isaiah's vision forms the epigraph of Silkin's first volume of poetry, *The Peaceable Kingdom* (1954), and remains a shared ideal for Gentiles and Jews:

"The wolf also shall dwell with the lamb, and the leopard shall lie down with the kid; and the calf and the young lion and the fatling together; and a little child shall lead them. And the cow and the bear shall feed; their young ones shall lie down together: and the lion shall eat straw like the ox. And the suckling child shall play on the hole of the asp, and the weaned child shall put his hand on the cockatrice'[s] den."

The local recurs as a theme for several of the poets included here. Dannie Abse, for example, describes "those sexy red-headed Pinskys/of Leeds" in 'Tales of Shatz'; Michael Horovitz visits London's former Jewish East End in 'Hard By Old Jewry', while Jonathan Treitel wittily transposes the legend of Rabbi Loew's Golem from sixteenth-century Prague to twentieth-century North London in 'The Golem of Golders Green' ("He is assigned commandments:/sweep the rabbi's floor; guard the Ghetto gate;/drop into Grodzinski's for a kilo of Israeli couscous in a cellophane bag;/pick up the usual at the Bagel Bakery...").

Elaine Feinstein's poems similarly emphasise a local habitation which is compatible with Jewishness ('Some Local Resistance', 'Dad', 'Some Thoughts on Where'). Her poem 'New Year' is set on "Rosh Hashonah, the New Year," in Cambridge, where Feinstein lived for many years. It poses a starkly Anglo-Jewish question: "How are we Jewish, and what brings us together/in this most puritan of Protestant centres?" The question revolves around a voluntary affiliation to Jewishness, in a place where oppressive laws are not forcing Jews to gather together. Possibly, the answer to it lies in the poet's search for some sort of existential authenticity. As Jean-Paul Sartre writes: "The inauthentic Jew flees Jewish reality, and the anti-Semite makes him a Jew in spite of himself; but the authentic Jew *makes himself a Jew*, in the face of all."[5]

(5)

A.C. Jacobs is the only Scottish poet featured in this anthology. His Scottish-Jewish sense of place is conveyed with typically tender humour in 'Place':

'Where do you come from?'
'Glasgow.'
'What part?'
'Vilna.'
'Where the heck's that?'
'A bit east of the Gorbals,
In around the heart.'

Born in what has been described as "a ghetto within a ghetto,"[6] Jacobs reacted by travelling widely, living in Spain, England, Italy and Israel. Several of his poems, such as 'Report', focus on Israeli-Palestinian relations. Jacobs also published translations of the Israeli poets David Vogel and Avraham Ben-Yitzhak. Despite the exceptional quality of Jacobs' translations from the Hebrew, I have chosen to include only original works in *Passionate Renewal*.

Interestingly, half of the poets here are, or were, translators. Jon Silkin co-translated Israeli poetry, principally by Natan Zach and Amir Gilboa. Daniel Weissbort is editor of the journal *Modern Poetry in Translation*, and has translated many Russian poets, including Nikolai Zabolotsky. Ruth Fainlight translates the Portuguese poet, Sophia de Mello Breyner, and the French poet, Jean Joubert. Christopher Ricks included a selection of Elaine Feinstein's translations from the Russian poet Marina Tsvetayeva in *The Oxford Book of English Verse* (1999). Dannie Abse has translated Pushkin. George Szirtes translates from the Hungarian; Michael Horovitz and Lotte Kramer from the German. Meanwhile, Michael Hamburger was awarded the German Federal Republic's Goethe Prize in 1986, and the EC's first European Translation Prize in 1990, for his work on a range of major German-language writers, including the Jewish poets Nelly Sachs and Paul Celan.

Ilan Stavans, editor of *The Oxford Book of Jewish Stories* (1998), has remarked "that Jewish literature is written as if already in translation."[7] Stavans' point is that Jewish literature *per se* is international, and therefore "translation is at the heart of the Jewish Diasporic experience."[8]

To be sure, translations by British Jewish poets display a concern with cultures outside the United Kingdom. While these poets extol the local, they refuse parochial insularity. One can risk a generalisation by proposing that British Jewish poets feel a kinship with specific places abroad, as well as their particular homes in these Isles.

Richard Burns, for example, makes frequent visits to Yugoslavia. His unfinished sequence of poems, 'The Blue Butterfly', is based on the massacre of seven thousand men and boys from the town of Kragujevac in Serbia on October 21, 1941. Burns told me that the sequence is unfinished because of "the continuing misery throughout Serbia and Kosovo,"[9] long after the Nazi occupiers have fled. The poem from the sequence reproduced here appeared in *The Jewish Quarterly*, when Burns won the Wingate-*Jewish Quarterly* Prize for Poetry in 1992. It begins in Jewish "ghettos and shtetls," and concludes universally with the poet's "international bloody human hand."

Burns has surely scored a first for British poetry by publishing a volume in Serbo-Croatian before it appears in English. A version of *The Manager* appeared in translation in Montenegro in 1990. It was only published in Britain in 2001.

(6)

History is a recurrent theme in British Jewish poetry. For the Jewish people, most of whom continue to reside in the diaspora, history remains a vital factor in constructing identity. Jews (and other minorities) need history to remind them who they are, particularly when the Gentile majority remain largely ignorant of what constitutes Jewish (and other minority groups') specificity.

In 1946 Emanuel Litvinoff, the most senior of the poets represented here, wrote in 'Earth and Eden':

> Where time and memory intersect the sun
> seeds of the wise tree grow about our roots;
> where space and conquest spread upon the earth
> our wisdom is undone.

Litvinoff emphasises "time and memory" as a juncture of future "seeds" and past "roots." This was universally applicable to a people without a permanent country, before the establishment of the State of Israel in 1948. Indeed, the poet links and censures "space and conquest" as antithetical to Jewish "wisdom." His perspective is that of a man who feels at home in Jewish culture and history, rather than any particular country.

Locating oneself with an historical anchor does not necessarily imply security. In Fainlight's 'Vertical', for example, the poet notes:

> It takes generations
> To breed such a true believer,
> Centuries to produce
> Someone who instinctively knew
> The only movement possible
> Was up or down. No space
> For me on the earth's surface.

This is the curse of an exilic Jewish time without space. However, there is also a blessing. The poet can define herself, "free/From whomsoever's definition:/Jew. Woman. Poet." She is empowered by language, finding her home in the texts she writes: "I am released by language,/I escape through speech."

One is reminded here of Silkin's comment about A.C. Jacobs: "Having a minority consciousness he could site himself nowhere. There was no home, except in his speech and written language."[10] Of course, one is also reminded that Jewish survival in the diaspora has traditionally depended on a collection of religious texts, the most important of these being the Torah (the first five books of the Old Testament). Such religious texts have provided diasporic Jews with a metaphorical home for two millennia.

In 'Seder Night with my Ancestors', Joanne Limburg recreates the rhythms of the Haggadah, the prayer book used to celebrate the Passover (Moses leading the Jews from slavery in Egypt to the Promised Land). Through a Judaic text, Limburg engages in a dialogue with her forebears. Her historical anchor, however, feels more like Coleridge's albatross around her neck:

At last I ask them:
What do you want from me?
What have you got to do with me?
Why do you come here, every year
on this night?

Her ancestors express similar exasperation at their Jewish plight:

They say:
For this God brought us forth from Egypt?
For this we starved in the desert?
For this we fled the inquisition?
For this we fled the pogroms?

11

All the generations, in Limburg's vision, are tied to the curse and celebration of Jewish history.

Passover proves inspirational for several poets as an annual celebration of Jewish perseverance and freedom. In this anthology, it provides the context for further poems by Jeremy Robson ('The Departure') and Bernard Kops ('Passover '38').

Outside of Israel, the *Pesach* (Passover) service ends with the prayer: "Next year in Jerusalem!" In Israel, the prayer is adapted to praise God for restoring Jerusalem to the Jews. Thus, each year British Jews express their ambivalent relationship to Israel. At *Pesach*, those of us who attend a service pray to return to Zion. However, the vast majority remain in Britain.

(7)

Some British Jewish poets have lived for varying lengths of time in Israel – notably, Jon Silkin, Karen Gershon and A.C. Jacobs – but all have returned home, to the diaspora. Several others have considered Israel, Jewish nationalism and the Arab-Israeli conflict. Emanuel Litvinoff sees the young country as "a marriage between youth and the soil," which may "unburden" Israelis of Jewish history ('For a New Generation'). Dannie Abse compares the Yiddish of the diaspora with the Hebrew of Israel in terms of a diasporic curse and a Zionistic blessing: "Say now in Yiddish:/'Exile. Pogrom. Wandering. Holocaust.'/Say now in Hebrew:/'Blessed Art Thou O Lord.'" ('Of Two Languages') Treitel notes the improvisational interaction between Israelis and their landscape in 'Tel Aviv Airport' ("And if there's nowhere in the vicinity remotely suitable –/no flatness for hundreds of miles, the entire/rugged country a crisscross of angled slopes –/the airport will be built somewhere somehow;" "And meanwhile the sesame ripens and is harvested"). Provocatively, Silkin suggests that the Arab-Israeli conflict has inverted the Passover story, with the Jews now the masters rather than the victims: "We're Jewish Pharoahs/Flicking water, whipping it" ('Jews without Arabs'). It is hard to find a consensus of opinion here, beyond the fact that all these poets care about Israel's character and future.

(8)

There may be Jewish masters in Israel, but some Jews in Britain equate Jewishness with victimhood. Philip Hobsbaum's poetry, for instance, repeatedly presents Jews as victims. To be sure, his vision is often parodic, for example when Jewish victims are contrasted with British Imperialistic aggressors: "The jews are worst. 'What are these Hebrews here?'/(A henchman comes and whispers.) 'Is that so?'/Out comes the whip again" ('Bulldog Drummond Fights Again'). However, there is also a hint of masochism in that "whip." In 'Professor Grottmann Explains Everything' we read: "The masochists must be/whipped and thrashed at pleasure." The sadistic "Professor" of the poem explains that suffering is for his Jewish friend's own good: "And, indeed, in so far as he is a masochist,/He must have enjoyed being unhappy." Overshadowing this masochistic perspective of Jewishness is the Holocaust, Hobsbaum's ironically accredited "University of Auschwitz."

Sickness and pain are perennial themes in Hobsbaum's work. In 'The Sick Lion', for example, we are shown a creature who is diametrically opposite to Judaism's proud Lion of Judah. Hobsbaum's animal is described in language which carries traces of anti-Jewish discourses; for example, the lion is seen to "blink vengefully at the gloom,/sullen and unconsoled." Further, the lion inhabits a world of "sickness" and "detachment." In 'The Sick Lion', Hobsbaum presents the consummate masochistic outsider, disengaged from cultural community, sadly passive and marginalised.

13

There is, however, another side to Hobsbaum's work. In 'Testimony', he compares the "miracle" of his "being given a voice" after "these barren years," with God's granting of a son to Sarah late in life (see Genesis 21:2). Hobsbaum's 'Watching and Waiting' also draws on the Bible, both in its language ("And should it come to pass;" "that heaven divorced from me") and its engagement with the Jewish messianic tradition of "hope" (repeated five times in sixteen lines) for future "peace" (recalling Isaiah's – and Silkin's – Peaceable Kingdom). Together with his accomplished craft and ironic humour, Hobsbaum's quasi-Judaic faith redeems his poetic voice and saves it from disappearing into the silence of despair.

(9)

Ironic humour occurs, too, in the work of Daniel Weissbort. Poems such as 'Memories of War', 'So English' and 'My Country' wryly evoke alienation in the midst of popular patriotism and mainstream Anglo-Jewish acculturation to English norms: "With nostalgia, I remember/'Onward Christian Soldiers' and/'To be a Pilgrim'" ('Memories of War'). Though the "nostalgia" here is real, so is its ironic incongruity for a Jew living through the Second World War.

Weissbort's 'The Name's Progress' wittily describes the name-changes the poet underwent at school during the War: "Weissbort, the name, was antipathetic./Later, I surmised/it was a corruption of/Weissbart or Weissbrot –/these were no better./For a while, though, I was Whitbord,/so very whinglish and whistleclean." Deftly, playfully, a sense of dislocation from English society and language is conveyed. Weissbort has remarked that he occupies a "situation between languages, as it were."[11] One might adopt George Szirtes' term, and characterise Weissbort's work as the poetry of social, cultural and linguistic "inbetweenness."

"My greatest difficulty with nationally or culturally rooted notions," Szirtes writes in his preface to *The Budapest File* (2000), "is that they inevitably exclude those who are migrants, floaters, drifters and shadows. I may envy the rooted but I cannot enter their territory." Szirtes's state of "inbetweenness" began in the wake of the 1956 Hungarian uprising, when his family was offered asylum in England. He was eight years old. Szirtes considers his poetry somehow "synthetic" because not rooted in "a local diction." However, he also maintains: "Poetry is always local. It is just that in this case – and in the case of other writers, indeed, I would suggest an increasing number of writers, those used to moving about from place to place without a secure notion of belonging – the notion of the local is rooted in the incidental. For diction we might well substitute form as some kind of driving necessity."

Szirtes is a master of form. His extended sonnet sequences include 'Portrait of my Father in an English Landscape', 'The Looking-Glass Dictionary', 'Travel Book' and (with thirteen rather than the sonnet's usual fourteen lines) 'Metro'. Excerpts from 'Metro', which explores the fate of Hungarian Jews following the Nazi occupation in 1944, are included here. There are also poems which evoke the sense of being, in England, "somewhere between two histories and two traditions."[12] 'Anthropomorphosis' describes an incident of racial prejudice directed against "two dark men:"

It was as if I'd seen it all before –
That long sail of spit arching over.
By my will I held it there, suspended
Between brick and mouth.

The "suspended" state with which Szirtes empathises here is a repeated motif of British Jewish poetry. We see it in Hamburger's 'Homeless', and it recurs, for example, in Abse's 'Street Scene' (where Jews in Golders Green are imagined "kicking as if under water") and Kramer's 'The Hour' (where a "kitchen's whiteness underneath/Hangs in a basement as suspended life"). Indeed, several British Jewish poets describe an ongoing sense of suspension between (in Szirtes' words) "the possibility of happiness" and an "apprehension of disaster."[13]

(10)

Happiness is clearly on the agenda of Michael Horovitz, Bernard Kops and Michael Rosen. As well as writing exciting poetry, Horovitz has been an indefatigable organiser of poetry celebrations since 1965, when he hosted (and read at) the first Poetry Olympics in the Albert Hall. As he explains in the 'Afterword' to his verse collection *Wordsounds and Sightlines* (1994), Jewishness is a major source of joy and inspiration. "Quite often in the midst of supra-national poetry events I find myself involuntarily imagining *yom tov* (a Jewish festival – literally 'good day')," he writes: "Our large-scale happenings and recitals, festivals and Poetry Olympics events at venues like London's Royal Albert Hall and Westminster Abbey have in fact seemed positively Biblic to some."

Like Limburg, Horovitz sometimes deploys Judaic prayer rhythms in his work; for example in the seven-part sequence 'Synagogue Music', part two of which is reproduced here.

Bernard Kops also associates his poetic vision with the religious "Yomtov." In 'Passover '38', he recalls "running that Yomtov gauntlet/of twisted cheeks and wet kisses." Behind the joy and humour here, as so often in Jewish literature, lies tragedy: "The Angel of Death? Who is he?/a madman on the radio, far away." That "madman" is Hitler. Similarly in 'Succot (Harvest Festival)', the "laughter" and "songs are the dreams/we capture from the dark."

Michael Rosen is perhaps best known as a children's writer. Indeed, the majority of the poems I have chosen here concern children and childhood experiences. Rosen's is an anecdotal, and often very funny, poetry. Occasionally, his work uses the Yiddish figure of the *schlemiel* (fool) to amuse ('The Wedding'). Frequently, his poems incorporate Yiddish words, such as *shmatte* (clothing of poor quality), *shul* (synagogue), *Zeyde* (grandfather) and *Bubbe* (grandmother). This is a linguistic sign of identification with the (formerly Yiddish-speaking) diaspora, rather than (modern Hebrew-speaking) Israel. Indeed, 'Burglary' features an anti-Zionist manifesto. "ANTI-ZIONIST IS NOT ANTI-SEMITIC," the poem quotes from banners carried by Stamford Hill *hassidim* (members of an ultra-orthodox Jewish sect).

Regarding antisemitism in English society ('New School') and literature ('English Literature'), Rosen is unflinchingly perceptive. He is also angry, as Emanuel Litvinoff was before him in his epoch-making poem 'To T.S. Eliot'.

Surrounding Litvinoff's poem is a story with the symmetry of a parable. In 1952 the poet was invited to read at the Institute of Contemporary Arts, in London. Litvinoff explains the historical and cultural context: "During the past week or so, I had written the Eliot poem. I remember buying his Penguin *Selected Poems*, and reading it on the train going home from work. I was working then for *The Jewish Observer*, and had these to review. And I was utterly appalled to read the poems that I knew he had written in the Twenties repeated here in his *Selected Poems*, after Auschwitz." These poems included 'Gerontion', 'Sweeney among the Nightingales' and 'Burbank with a Baedeker: Bleistein with a Cigar', all of which are antisemitic.[14]

Litvonoff resolved to read 'To T.S. Eliot' at the ICA. Just as he was about to begin, Eliot walked into the room. Litvinoff told me: "I nearly died. Apparently, Eliot had arrived with an entourage. I thought: well, I'll have to read it. And I read the poem, and it absolutely stunned everybody." Accusations started flying that the poem was "libellous, slanderous!" [15] According to Dannie Abse, who remembers being seated in front of Eliot, the latter put "his head down" after the reading, and "muttered generously, 'It's a good poem; it's a very good poem'."[16]

(11)

Half of the poets in this anthology are themselves anthologists. Dannie Abse has edited a variety of anthologies over the years, including *Mavericks* (1957, with Howard Sergeant), *The Hutchinson Book of Post-War English Poetry* (1989) and *Twentieth Century Anglo-Welsh Poetry* (1997). Philip Hobsbaum co-edited *The Group Anthology* of contemporary poets in 1963. Michael Horovitz's anthologies include *Children of Albion* (1969), *Grandchildren of Albion* (1990) and *The Poetry Olympics Party Anthology* (2000). Bernard Kops edited *Poetry Hounslow* in 1981, and Emanuel Litvinoff *The Penguin Book of Jewish Short Stories* in 1979. Both Gerda Mayer's *Poet Tree Centaur: A Walthamstow Group Anthology* and Jeremy Robson's *Modern Poets in Focus* appeared in 1973. Among Michael Rosen's several international anthologies of children's poetry and fiction are *A World of Poetry* (1994) and *Funny Stories* (1993). Jon Silkin's anthology, *Poetry of the Committed Individual*, appeared in 1973. A few years later, Silkin edited *The Penguin Book of First World War Poetry* (1979). Daniel Weissbort's anthologies include *Post-War Russian Poetry* (1974) and *The Poetry of Survival: Post-War Poets of Central and Eastern Europe* (1990).

Why has the compiling of anthologies proved so popular with British Jewish poets? I would suggest, on the basis of personal experience, that such poets are arguing for a literary context in which they feel they have a place – albeit unfixed – both in tradition and contemporary practice. The aim of *Passionate Renewal*, similarly, is to map literary locations for poets and poetry readers alike.

I wish to thank Ross Bradshaw, from Five Leaves, for his unflagging support and encouragement over the two years in which this book has been in preparation. Thanks are

18

also due to Anthony Rudolf for his astute editorial advice and for sharing his knowledge of Jewish poets. From the inception of *Passionate Renewal*, Anthony has offered the wisdom and experience of a seasoned anthologist. My appreciation of the help offered by Professor Bryan Cheyette and Professor Dan Jacobson similarly merits mention. Both men kindly appraised early drafts of my introduction. Much of the work for *Passionate Renewal* was conducted at the Poetry Library in London, and I wish to express my gratitude to all Library staff for their cheerful assistance.

Peter Lawson
January 2001

Notes

[1] See Hana Wirth-Nesher, 'Defining the Indefinable: What Is Jewish Literature?', in *What Is Jewish Literature?* (The Jewish Publication Society, 1994), pp.3-12.

[2] Paul Fussell, *The Great War and Modern Memory* (OUP, 1975), p.250.

[3] *Voices Within the Ark: The Modern Jewish Poets*, eds. Anthony Rudolf and Howard Schwartz (Avon, 1980), p.395.

[4] 'Interview: Jon Silkin', *Sphagnum* 11 (1981), pp.24-33.

[5] Jean-Paul Sartre, *Anti-Semite and Jew*, trans. George J. Becker, (1946; Schocken, 1948), p.137.

[6] Gerald Mangan reviewing Ralph Glasser's *A Gorbals Legacy; Times Literary Supplement*, August 11, 2000, p.8.

[7] *The Jewish Quarterly*, Autumn 1999, pp.47-52.

[8] Ibid., p.47.

[9] E-mail correspondence between Richard Burns and Peter Lawson.

[10] Jon Silkin, 'Arthur Jacobs, Poet', in Arthur C. Jacobs, *Collected Poems & Selected Translations* (Menard/Hearing Eye, 1996).

[11] *Contemporary Poets* (St James Press, 1996), p.1178.

[12] Ibid., p.1098.

[13] Ibid., p.1097.

[14] For a discussion of these poems, see Maud Ellmann, 'The Imaginary Jew: T.S. Eliot and Ezra Pound', *Between "Race" and Culture: Representations of "the Jew" in English and American Literature*, edited by Bryan Cheyette (Stanford University Press,

1996), pp.84-101. See also Bryan Cheyette, *Constructions of 'The Jew' in English Literature and Society: Racial Representations, 1875-1945* (Cambridge University Press, 1993), pp.234-267. For an overview of Eliot's work, see Anthony Julius, *T.S. Eliot, Anti-Semitism, and Literary Form* (Cambridge University Press, 1995).

[15] Emanuel Litvinoff in conversation with Peter Lawson (unpublished), November 21, 1999.

[16] Dannie Abse, *A Poet in the Family* (Hutchinson, 1974), pp.130-132.

Dannie Abse

Odd

In front of our house in Golders Green
the lawn, like a cliché, mutters, 'Rose bushes.'
The whole suburb is very respectable.
Ugly men drive past in funeral suits,
from their necks you can tell they're overweight.

Sodium lamp-posts, at night, hose empty roads
with gold which treacles over pavement trees,
polishes brittle hedges, clings on closed, parked cars.
If a light should fly on in an upstairs room
odds on two someones are going to sleep.

It's unusual to meet a beggar,
you hardly ever see a someone drunk.
It's a nice, clean, quiet, religious place.
For my part, now and then, I want to scream:
thus, by the neighbours, am considered odd.

From the sensible wastes of Golders Green
I journey to Soho where a job owns me.
Soho is not a respectable place.
Underweight women in the gamiest of skirts
bleed a smile of false teeth at ugly men.

Later, the dark is shabby with paste electric
of peeporamas, brothels, clubs and pubs,
restaurants that sport sallow waiters who cough.
If a light should fly on in an upstairs room
odds on two someones are going to bed.

It's customary to see many beggars,
common to meet people roaring and drunk.
It's a nice, loud, dirty, irreligious place.
For my part, now and then, I want to scream:
thus, by Soho friends, am considered odd.

After the Release of Ezra Pound

In Jerusalem I asked
the ancient Hebrew poets to forgive you,
and what would Walt Whitman have said
and Thomas Jefferson?
                    (Paul Potts)

In Soho's square mile of unoriginal sin
where the fraudulent neon lights haunt,
but cannot hide, the dinginess of vice,
the jeans and sweater boys spoke of Pound,
and you, Paul, repeated your question.

The chee-chee bums in Torino's laughed and
the virgins of St Martin's School of Art.
The corner spivs with their Maltese masks
loitered for the two o'clock result,
and those in the restaurants of Greek Street,
eating income tax, did not hear the laugh.

Gentle Gentile, you asked the question.
Free now (and we praise this) Pound could answer.

The strip lighting of Soho did not fuse,
no blood trickled from a certain book
down the immaculate shelves of Zwemmer's.
But the circumcised did not laugh.
The swart nudes in the backrooms put on clothes
and the doors of the French pub closed.

Pound did not hear the raw Jewish cry,
the populations committed to the dark
when he muttered through microphones
of murderers. He, not I, must answer.

Because of the structures of a beautiful poet
you ask the man who is less than beautiful,
and wait in the public neurosis of Soho,
in the liberty of loneliness for an answer.

In the beer and espresso bars they talked
of Ezra Pound, excusing the silences of an old man,
saying there is so little time between
the parquet floors of an institution
and the boredom of the final box.

Why, Paul, if that ticking distance between
was merely a journey long enough
to walk the circumference of a Belsen,
Walt Whitman would have been eloquent,
and Thomas Jefferson would have cursed.

A Night Out

Friends recommended the new Polish film
at the Academy in Oxford Street.
So we joined the ever melancholy queue
of cinemas. A wind blew faint suggestions
of rain towards us, and an accordion.
Later, uneasy, in the velvet dark
we peered through the cut-out oblong window
at the spotlit drama of our nightmares:
images of Auschwitz almost authentic,
the human obscenity in close-up.
Certainly we could imagine the stench.

Resenting it, we forgot the barbed wire
was but a prop and could not scratch an eye;
those striped victims merely actors like us.
We saw the Camp orchestra assembled,
we heard the solemn gaiety of Bach,
scored by the loud arrival of an engine,
its impotent cry and its guttural trucks.
We watched, as we munched milk chocolate,
trustful children, no older than our own,
strolling into the chambers without fuss,
while smoke, black and curly, oozed from chimneys.

Afterwards, at a loss, we sipped coffee
in a bored espresso bar nearby
saying very little. You took off one glove.
Then to the comfortable suburb swiftly
where, arriving home, we garaged the car.
We asked the au pair girl from Germany
if anyone had phoned at all, or called,
and, of course, if the children had woken.
Reassured, together we climbed the stairs,
undressed together, and naked together,
in the dark, in the marital bed, made love.

White Balloon

Dear love, Auschwitz made me
more of a Jew than Moses did.
But the world's not always with us.
Happiness enters here again tonight
like an unexpected guest
with no memory of the future either;

enters with such an italic emphasis,
jubilant, announcing triumphantly
hey presto and here I am and opening
the June door into our night living room
where, under the lampshade's ciliate,
an armchair's occupied by a white balloon.
As if there'd been a party.

Of course, Happiness, uninhibited,
will pick it up, his stroking thumb
squeaking a little as he leads us to the hall.
And we shall follow him, too,
when he climbs the lit staircase
towards the landing's darkness,
bouncing bouncing the white balloon
from hand to hand.

It's bedtime; soon we must dream
separately — but what does it matter now
as the white balloon is thrown up high?
Quiet, so quiet, the moon above Masada
and closed, abandoned for the night,
the icecream van at Auschwitz.

Demo against the Vietnam War, 1968

Praise just one thing in London, he challenged,
as if everybody, everything, owned a minus,
was damnable, and the Inner Circle led to hell;
and I thought, allowed one slot only,
what, in October, would I choose?

Not the blurred grasslands of a royal, moody park
where great classy trees lurk in mist;
not the secretive Thames either, silvering
its slow knots through the East End —
sooty scenes, good for Antonioni panning soft
atmospheric shots, emblems of isolation,
prologue to the elegiac Square, the house where,
suddenly, lemon oblongs spring to windows.

Nor would I choose the stylised catalogue
of torment in the National Gallery.
Better that tatty group, under Nelson's column,
their home-made banners held aloft,
their small cries of 'Peace, Peace,' impotent;
also the moment with the tannoy turned off,
the thudding wings of pigeons audible,
the shredding fountains, once again, audible.

So praise to the end of the march,
their songs, their jargon, outside the Embassy.
Yes, this I'd choose: their ardour, their naïveté,
violence of commitment, cruelty of devotion,
'We shall not be moved, We shall overcome' —
despite sullen police concealed in vans
waiting for arclights to fail, for furtive darkness,
and camera-teams, dismantled, all breezing home.

27

Car Journeys*

1. Down the M4

Me! dutiful son going back to South Wales, this time afraid
to hear my mother's news. Too often, now,
                              her friends are disrobed,
and my aunts and uncles, too, go into the hole, one by one.
The beautiful face of my mother is in its ninth decade.

Each visit she tells me the monotonous story of clocks.
'Oh dear,' I say, or 'how funny,' till I feel my hair
                              turning grey
for I've heard that perishable one two hundred times
    before –
like the rugby 'amateurs' with golden sovereigns in
                              their socks.

Then the Tawe ran fluent and trout-coloured over
                              stones stonier,
more genuine; then Annabella, my mother's mother,
    spoke Welsh
with such an accent the village said, 'Tell the truth, fach,
you're no Jewess. *They're* from the Bible. *You're*
                              from Patagonia!'

I'm driving down the M4 again under bridges that leap
over me then shrink in my side mirror. Ystalyfera is farther
than smoke and God further than all distance known.
    I whistle
no hymn but an old Yiddish tune my mother knows.
    It won't keep.

*This poem is from a four-part sequence.

The Weeping

After I lean from my shadow
to switch on the dark in the lamp,
I sense distant riders
and a disembodied crone-voice rasping,
'Do not weep like a woman
for what you would not fight for as a man.'
Eyes closed before sleep
I think how sleep is a going into exile;
how shadows also
are but cut-out pieces of darkness
exiled from darkness.
(Each summer's day especially,
the diaspora of shadows
awaits the return of night.)

Already, clearly, I hear the advance
of horses, their regular pounding.
Soon two shadows on horseback appear:
one Boabdil, a king long dead,
the other, his scolding mother.
What is dream, what is not dream?
They ride round the corner
of night. They loom near
and become substance. They halt
their horses. They look back
at the alhambra of fable.
(Years since I, a tourist, sauntered
in the alhambra of fable,
read their guidebook story).

Not the most woeful sound a man may hear,
an exile weeping and weeping.
Yet desolate it is
like a ram's horn blown
in a hushed synagogue,
like Christian bells opening, closing,

like the muezzin heard
even after he has ceased.
Such is the sound this man makes
looking back with clarifying remorse.
No man weeping either,
but a silhouette of a man,
a hunched shadow on horseback,
a homeless shadow weeping.

  And I wake up
weeping. I and another both weep
in the darkness, weep in unison.
I wake up. I sit up and stop weeping.
  No-one weeps.

Tales of Shatz

Meet Rabbi Shatz in his correct black homburg.
The cheder boys call him Ginger.
If taller than 5 foot you're taller than he;
also taller than his father,
grandfather, great grandfather.

Meet Ruth Shatz, née Ruth Pinsky,
short-statured too, straight-backed.
In her stockinged feet
her forehead against his,
her eyes smile into his.
And again on the pillow, later.
Ah those sexy red-headed Pinskys
of Leeds and Warsaw: her mother,
grandmother, great grandmother!

Mrs Shatz resembles Rabbi Shatz's mother.
Rabbi Shatz resembles Mrs Shatz's father.
Strangers mistake them for brother, sister.

At University, Solly Shatz, their morning star,
suddenly secular, all 6 foot of him —
a black-haired centre-forward on Saturdays —
switches studies from Theology to Genetics.

*

A certain matron of Golders Green,
fingering amber beads about her neck,
approaches Rabbi Shatz.
When I was a small child, she thrills,
once, just once, God the Holy One
came through the curtains of my bedroom.
What on earth has he been doing since?

Rabbi Shatz turns, he squints,
he stands on one leg
hoping for the inspiration of a Hillel.
The Holy One, he answers, blessed be He,
has been waiting, waiting patiently,
till you see Him again.

*

Consider the mazzle of Baruch Levy
who changed his name to Barry Lee,
who moved to Esher, Surrey,
who sent his four sons Matthew, Mark,
Luke and John to boarding school,
who had his wife's nose fixed,
who, blinking in the Gents,
turned from the writing on the wall
and later, still blinking, joined the golf club.

With new friend, Colonel Owen,
first game out, under vexed clouds,
thunder detonated without rain,
lightning stretched without thunder,
and near the 2nd hole,
where the darker green edged
to the shaved lighter green,
both looked up terrified.
Barbed fire zagged towards them
to strike dead instantly
Mostyn Owen, Barry Lee's opponent.
What luck that Colonel Owen
(as Barry discovered later)
once was known as Moshe Cohen.

*

Now, continued Rabbi Shatz,
recall how even the sorrows of Job
had a happy ending.

Being a religious man Shatz adored riddles.
Who? he asked his impatient wife.

Who like all men came into this world
with little fists closed, departed
with large hands open, yet on walking
over snow and away from sunsets
followed no shadow in front of him,
left no footprint behind him?

You don't know either, opined his wife.
You and your Who? Who?
Are you an owl?
Why do you always pester me with riddles
you don't know the answer of?

Rabbi Shatz for some reason wanted to cry.
If I knew the answers, he whispered,
would my questions still be riddles?
And he tiptoed away, closed the door
so softly behind him
as if on a sleeping dormitory.

Often when listening to music
before a beautiful slow movement
recaptured him, Shatz would blank out,
hear nothing. So now, too, in his lit study
as night rain tilted outside
across dustbins in the lane
he forgot why his lips moved, his body swayed.

Lunch with a Pathologist

My colleague knows by heart the morbid verse
of facts — the dead weight of a man's liver,
a woman's lungs, a baby's kidneys.

At lunch he recited unforgettably,
'After death, of all soft tissues the brain's
the first to vanish, the uterus the last.'

'Yes,' I said, 'at dawn I've seen silhouettes
hunched in a field against the skyline, each one
feasting, preoccupied, silent as gas.

Partial to women they've stripped women bare,
and left behind only the taboo food,
the uterus, inside the skeleton.'

My colleague wiped his mouth with a napkin,
hummed, picked shredded meat from his canines,
said, 'You're a peculiar fellow, Abse.'

Of Itzig and His Dog

To pray for the impossible,
says Itzig, is disgraceful.
I prefer, when I'm on my own,
when I'm only with my dog,
when I can't go out
because of the weather,
because of my shoes,
to talk very intimately to God.

Itzig, they nag, why do that,
what's the point of that?
God never replies surely?

Such ignorance! Am I at the Western Wall?
Am I on spacious Mount Sinai?
Is there a thornbush in this murky room?
God may never say a word,
may never even whisper, Itzig, hullo.

But when I'm talking away
to the right and to the left,
when it's raining outside,
when there's rain on the glass,
when I say please God this
and thank God that,
then God always makes, believe me,
the dog's tail wag.

Street Scene
(Outside the grocer's, Golders Green Road)

They quarrel, this black-bearded man
and his busy, almost flying wife —
she with her hands, he with proverbs.

'He who never rebukes his son,'
says the bearded man too blandly,
'leads him into delinquency.'

And she who hasn't studied nicely
such studied wisdom, now replies,
'You're a, you're a, you're a donkey.'

Three or four psychiatrists smile
as they pass the greengrocer's shop.
Again, patient, he quotes the Talmud:

'When one suggests you're a donkey
do not fret; only when two speak thus
go buy yourself a saddle.'

But she has thrown appropriate
carrots carrots at his sober head
and one sticks brightly in his beard.

Truce! You have been led into fiction.
Listen! Here comes a violin
and tunes to make a donkey dance.

The bearded man has closed his eyes.
Who's this, disguised as a beggar,
playing a violin without strings?

What music's this, its cold measure?
Who are these, dangling from lampposts,
kicking as if under water?

In the Holiday Inn

After the party I returned to the hotel.
The room was too hot so I took off my coat.

It was January but I turned down the thermostat.
I took off my shirt but I was still too hot.

I opened the window, it was snowing outside.
Despite all this the air began to simmer.

The room had a pyrexia of unknown origin.
I took off my trousers, I took off my shorts.

This room was a cauldron, this room was tropical.
On the wall, the picture of willows changed

to palm trees. In the mirror I could see the desert.
I stood naked in my socks and juggled

with pomegranates. I offered offerings
that soon became burnt. This was some holiday.

I took off one sock and read the bible.
They were cremating idols, sacrificing oxen.

I could feel the heat of their fiery furnace.
I could hear those pyromaniacs chanting.

I could smell the singed wings of cherubim.
I took off the other sock and began to dance.

Like sand the carpet scalded my twinkling feet.
Steam was coming out of both my ears.

I was King David dancing before the Lord.
Outside it was snowing but inside it was Israel.

37

I danced six cubits this way, six cubits that.
Now at dawn I'm hotter than the spices of Sheba.

What shall I do? I shall ask my wise son,
Solomon. Where are you Solomon?

You are not yet born, you do not know
how wise you are or that I'm your father

and that I'm dancing and dancing.

Case History

'Most Welshmen are worthless,
an inferior breed, doctor.'
He did not know I was Welsh.
Then he praised the architects
of the German death-camps —
did not know I was a Jew.
He called liberals, 'White blacks',
and continued to invent curses.

When I palpated his liver
I felt the soft liver of Goering;
when I lifted my stethoscope
I heard the heartbeats of Himmler;
when I read his encephalograph
I thought, '*Sieg heil, mein Führer.*'

In the clinic's dispensary
red berry of black bryony,
cowbane, deadly nightshade, deathcap.
Yet I prescribed for him
as if he were my brother.

Later that night I must have slept
on my arm: momentarily
my right hand lost its cunning.

Of Two Languages
(for Hanoch Bartov)

1
Citizen Dov walking on Mount Carmel
heard Agnon speaking Yiddish to a companion.
'How can you,' complained Dov, 'a five-star scholar,
a great *Hebrew* author, a Nobel prize winner,
prophet amongst men, Solomon amongst Kings,
a genuine, first-class somebody (destined for
a state funeral) how can *you* speak Yiddish?'

'Observe which way we're walking,' replied Agnon.
'Downhill. Downhill, I always speak Yiddish.
Uphill — break forth into singing, ye mountains —
uphill, I speak the language of Isaiah.'

2
Dov, you know Hebrew, you also know Yiddish.
Did you not speak to God in Hebrew
when you spoke to men in Yiddish?
All those used-up, ascetic centuries
of studying the evidence of 22 consonants;
the 23rd would not have destroyed the world.

Now in Hebrew, bellicose, you say, 'Go away.'
Once, softly in Yiddish, you begged, 'Leave me alone.'
Tell me, what's the word for 'mercy' in Hebrew?
In Yiddish, 'mercy' must have many synonyms.

Say now in Yiddish:
'Exile. Pogrom. Wandering. Holocaust.'
Say now in Hebrew:
'Blessed Art Thou O Lord.'

Snake

When the snake bit
Rabbi Hanina ben Dosa
while he was praying

the snake died. (Each day
is attended by surprises
or it is nothing.)

Question: was the bare-footed,
smelly Rabbi more poisonous
than the snake

or so God-adulterated
he'd become immune
to serpent poison?

Oh great-great-great-uncles,
your palms weighing air,
why are you arguing?

Listen, the snake thought
(being old and unwell
and bad-tempered as hell)

Death, where's thy sting?
In short, was just testing:
a snake's last fling.

Yes, the *so-called* snake
was dying anyway, its heart
calcified and as old as Eden.

No, that snake was A1 fit
but while hissing for fun it
clumsily bit its own tongue.

41

No, Hanina invented that snake;
not for his own sake but for first-
class, religious publicity.

No no, here's the key to it.
Ask: did the Rabbi, later on,
become a jumpy, timid man?

Remember, he who has been bitten
by a snake thereafter becomes
frightened of a rope . . .

Bearded men in darkening rooms
sipping lemon tea and arguing
about the serpent till the moon

of Russia, of Latvia, Lithuania,
Poland, rose above the alien
steeples — centuries of sleep.

Now, tonight, a clean-shaven rabbi
who once studied in Vienna
says snake-venom contains

haemolysins, haemo-
coagulants, protolysins,
cytolysins and neurotoxins

and that even in Hanina
ben Dosa's day a snake was a
snake unless, of course, it was

a penis, an unruly penis,
making a noise like one pissing
on a mound of fresh hot ashes.

Oh great-great-great-uncles
did you hear him? And are your
handbones weighing moonshine?

O Taste and See

Because of a kiss on the forehead
in the long Night's infirmary,
through the red wine let light shine deep.

Because of the thirtysix just men
that so stealthily roam this earth
raise high the glass and do not weep.

Who says the world is not a wedding?
Couples, in their oases, lullabye.
Let glass be full before they sleep.

Toast all that which seems to vanish
like a rainbow stared at, those bright
truant things that will not keep;

and ignorance of the last night
of our lives, its famished breathing.
Then, in the red wine, taste the light.

At the Albert Hall

Anarchic dissonances first, so that
somewhere else a lonely scarecrow shivers
in a winter field. A mortician's crow
perches on its head. It begins to snow.
They bring the scarecrow indoors. They feed it
with phosphorus so it should glow at night.
A great orchestra's tuning-up is ghost talk.

The wand! Then the sudden tamed silence of
a cemetery. Who dares to blackly cough?
Threatened, the conductor raises both arms,
an invisible gun pressed to his back.
Listen. And they speak of the sweet psalmist
of Israel, of 200 loaves of bread
and of 100 bundles of raisins.

My Neighbour, Itzig

My neighbour, Itzig,
has gone queer with religion.
Yesterday he asked me
who named the angels!

Today his dog is barking and barking.

But like music that's ceased
in an adjoining room
Itzig is not here.
He is nowhere else, either.

Itzig, listen, your dog needs a walk.

But Itzig is droning on and on
– open the window, someone –
a prayer archaic and musty
and full of O.

His sad feet are on this earth,
his happy head is elsewhere
among the configuration
of the 7 palaces of light.

Come back, Itzig, your dog needs feeding.

But Itzig quests for the 8th colour.
His soul is cartwheeling, he's far
from the barely manageable
drama of the Present Tense.

Come back, Itzig, your dog needs water.

But Itzig follows, with eyes closed,
the footsteps of the sages
Amora and Rehumai
who never existed.

A Letter from Ogmore-by-Sea

Goodbye, 20th Century.
What should I mourn?
Hiroshima? Auschwitz?
Our friend, Carmi, said,
'Thank forgetfulness
else we could not live;
thank memory
else we'd have no life.'

Goodbye, 20th Century.
What shall I celebrate?
Darling, I'm out of date:
even my nostalgia
is becoming history.
Those garish, come-on posters
outside a cinema,
announce the Famous
I've never heard of.
So many other friends, too,
now like Carmi, have joined
a genealogy of ghosts.

But here, this mellow evening,
on these high cliffs I look down
to read the unrolling
holy scrolls of the sea. They are
blank. The enigma is alive
and, for the Present, I boast,
thumbs in lapels, I survive.

Delightful Eros
still hauls Reason along
zig-zag on a taut leash.
I'm still unsettled by
the silence in framed pictures,
foreground and background;
or the mastery of music
over mind. And I hail
the world within a word.
I do not need to be
a fabulist like Iolo
who, from this same coast,
would see seven sails
where there was but one.

Goodbye, 20th Century,
your trumpets and your drums,
your war-wounds still unhealed.
Goodbye, I-must-leave-you-Dolly,
goodbye Lily Marlene.
Has the Past always a future?
Will there always be
a jackboot on the stair,
a refugee to roam?
A man with no roots is lost
like the darkness in the forest
and it costs 100 years
for a hiding place
to become a home.

Now secular strangers come
sealed in Fords and Nissans,
a congregation of cars,
to this opening estuary
so various, so beautiful, so old.
The tide is out.
And from the sleeping reeled-
in sea – not from
the human mind's vexed fathoms –
the awakened, eternal, murderous,
fanged Tusker Rock is revealed.

The Abandoned

There is no space unoccupied by the Shekinah

The Talmud

...thy absence doth excel
All distance known

George Herbert

1
God, when you came to our house
   we let you in. Hunted,
      we gave you succour,
         bandaged your hands,
            bathed your feet.

Wanting water we gave you wine.
Wanting bread we gave you meat.

Sometimes, God, you should recall
   we are your hiding-place.
      Take away these hands
         and you would fall.

Outside, the afflicted pass.
   We only have to call.
      They would open you
         with crutch and glass.

Who else then could we betray
   if not you, the nearest?
      God, how you watch us
         and shrink away.

2

Never have we known you so transparent.
You stand against the curtain and wear
its exact design. And if a window opens
(like a sign) then is it you
or the colours that are blown apart?

You startle from room to room, apologising.

God, you can't help your presence
any more than the glassy air that lies
between tree and skies. No need to pass
through wave-lengths human ears can't sense.

We never hear the front door close when you are leaving.
Sometimes we question if you are there at all.
No need to be so self-effacing;
quiet as language of the roses
or moss upon a wall.

We have to hold our breath to hear you breathing.

3

Dear God in the end you had to go.
Dismissing you, your absence made us sane.
We keep the bread and wine for show.

The white horse galloped across the snow,
melted, leaving no hoofmarks in the rain.
Dear God, in the end you had to go.

The winds of war and derelictions blow,
howling across the radioactive plain.
We keep the bread and wine for show.

Sometimes what we do not know we know –
who can count the stars, call each one by name?
Dear God in the end you had to go.

Yet boarding the last ship out all sorrow
that grape is but grape and grain is grain.
We keep the bread and wine for show.

Soon night will be like feathers of the crow,
small lights upon the shore begin to wane.
Dear God in the end you had to go,
we keep the bread and wine for show.

4
Now, God, you are the colour black.
Who prays, 'Come down, Thou, come down?'
Absurd saints search for the rack.
Omnipotence is what you lack
even when you stumble back.

Did you weep when you found us out?
Did you return to blaspheme
cursing Man? (Then should we be devout?)
Already you begin to doubt
if you really heard us shout.

It was your own voice, God, that cried.
Sulky, you thrust back the bolt
against the human noise outside.
Oh open the dammed door wide
Maybe someone dear has died.

Listen. Can't you hear again
an idiot desperate in a house,
the strict economy of pain,
a voice pleading and profane
calling you by name?

Richard Burns

The Blue Butterfly*

On my Jew's hand, born out of ghettos and shtetls,
Raised from unmarked graves of my obliterated people
In Germany, Latvia, Lithuania, Poland, Russia,

On my hand mothered by a refugee's daughter,
First opened in blitzed London, grown big
Through post-war years safe in suburban England,

On my pink, educated, ironical left hand
Of a parvenu not quite British pseudo gentleman
Which first learned to scrawl its untutored messages

Among Latin-reading rugby-playing militarists
In an élite boarding school on Sussex's green downs
And against the cloister walls of puritan Cambridge,

On my hand weakened by anomie, on my
Writing hand, now of a sudden willingly
Stretched before me in Serbian spring sunlight,

On my unique living hand, trembling and troubled
By this May visitation, like a virginal
Leaf new sprung on the oldest oak in Europe,

On my proud firm hand, miraculously
Blessed by the seven thousand martyred
Men and boys fallen at Kragujevac,

A blue butterfly simply fell out of the sky
And settled on the forefinger
Of my international bloody human hand.

This poem is part of an unfinished sequence.

The Manager (extracts)
31

She's watching *The Holocaust* smoking and paring back her cuticles glued to Episode Six. During the break it's

Wail Meat. A well meant bonus for Pussikins. For owners of fur skins and foreskins. Oh wettened white maid, well made

For purse-value, for purr-valour: How smooth runs The New Principessa. On AMGLO Grade Z Oil. Bulletin, Bully Tin, Bullet In:

Word-salad out of deep freeze with microwave image-broth, set alight by satellite across the wheeled wild world: The New

American Bible in authoritative translation, with a free statue of God cradling The Infant Baba in gold-plated plaster

From Bee Cheese: twice as nutritious as honey but half the calories. Grate it, slice it, toast it. Or melt it, whiter

Than white. See our beaches, our islands. Timeless masterpieces. Waiting. For You. Now. Holiday in Mamaia. Final solution

To all your washing problems. Our apocalyptic message will change your kitchen forever. For Purity, The Choice

Is Now Uniquely Yours. Take it, today, with MAPLAN. Sign your life-sentence to Top Security. To strains of

Hack-Up-Your-Doubles-In-An-Old-Bitch-Hag, and Devotional Hours to Wall Street, Bonn, Bruxelles, Tokyo, Zurich,

Walls taller than Berlin's blockade us, each from each. Lock us out from speech. Till bed-time when, beseeching

Rattling bodies reach. To Cape Town then I came. O Lord Thou. Dresden Nagasaki Sarajevo. Burning Burning Burning.

There go the dead again. Wailing. Constantly I hear them. Even when not listening. Even this side the partition wall.

Giggling in the office during coffee break. Conversing on the tube at the other end of the carriage. Beneath your voice on the phone.

In a meths drinker's snore from a bench on Platform 8. Whispering through the stadium under the crowd's roar. Crackling through gaps

In The Ultimate in CD Hi-Fi Integration. Despite metal particle coating lasers and microchips. Like a horde of Hollywood extras

In a multi-million epic. Like patients interminably queuing in the long term ward. Like camp inmates trudging into the chamber

Of showers. Like an army of giant ants endlessly on the move. From hole to hole. Cell to cell. Street to street. Block to block.

City to city. From one hell to another. Under the human buzz. Under the rattle of wheels. Under the traffic drone. Constantly I hear

The dead lamenting Jerusalem. Albion's most sophisticated hot-time swinger. Pretty brunette 34-24-35 wants to exchange ideas and photos

With men with big problems. Will also model for same. Enjoys Pyjama Parties/O/Vib/Blowi Fans. Your place or mine. London or anywhere.

That's when she's off-duty doing overtime on the side. Otherwise trusty PA to Sir Keith W Lawdon. Prospect's Chairman of the Board.

President of the CBI. Adviser to the Board of Trade. Who lives on Bishop's Avenue. And is worth at least six million.

89

Auntie Mimi has died leaving a full freezer. Frozen bones for stock. Stews for a rainy day. Half a kilo of home-made meat-balls flavoured with oregano. Her favourite apple pie, heavily spiced with cloves.

And we who have inherited, what should we do with this goodness? Sling it away, waste it? Bury it all with her? Or eat it, remembering her, since she with her love prepared it?

Five white cut loaves. Two mini-baguettes. Boiled gefilte fish. An unsliced hunk of salt beef. Unused packets of crumpets and dried filo pastry. An opened bag of prawns – oy oy. Peas. Beans. Sweetcorn.

Come, let us feast together, family and friends. For what we are about to receive, may the Lord make us jewly thankful. *Baruch ata Adonai, Elohanu melech ha'olom, ha'motsi lechem min ha aretz.*

Ruth Fainlight

Fever Hospital

The fever pustules first appear
in creases and the hidden parts.
The war is far away, I am safe here.
I sit at home. I live where there is peace.
My child plays submarines and guns
Though I discourage him. But every day
He senses what I read in the newspapers.
Perhaps he knows more than I do.
He trains himself for his expected future.

The fever symptoms break in me
As fascination with destructiveness.
I watch those whom I think my opposites,
Ignore complexities, and let them act
What I am too fastidious
To execute myself: those drenching
Surges of maliciousness, the dreams
Of torture (though I disinfect
My fantasy by playing victim).

If I must purge myself of fever
By surrogates: the monkey-man,
The Fascist, the monopolist, even
The householder and his dull omissions,
I spread the sickness just as much.
I mould the world as if I pressed
My form into a bed of wax
And called that shape my opposite;
As if external evil makes me good.
The country is at peace, at least I claim
That I am, though my dreams are troubled.

59

My child imagines dangers everywhere,
Demands to know the natural weapons
Of each creature, its protection.
For he was born into this fever hospital
And learns geography to make quite sure
Just where the tanks and airplanes are
Enacting the realities of power
Which I try to disclaim. It is no good.
The fever breeds within my blood.
This hectic flush must signal quarantine
To every corner of the universe.

Lilith

Lilith, Adam's first companion,
Assumed her equality.
For this she was banished.

God had created her
From the same earth as Adam.
She stood her ground, amazed
By the idea of differences.

Adam and God were embarrassed,
Humiliated. It was true –
They had been formed
At the same time, the two
Halves of His reflection.

Her expectations
Should have seemed justified.
But Adam needed to understand God.
A creature must now worship him,
Constrained and resentful as he.
God encouraged him.

To guard His mystery, God
Made Adam swoon.
There, when he awoke,
Awaited Eve, the chattel.

Eyes downcast, his phallus
The first thing she noticed.
The snake reminded her of it.

The nagging ache in his side
Where the rib was extracted
(In memory of which
The soldier thrust his spear)
Keeps Adam irritable.

Lilith's disgrace thus defined
Good and evil. She would be
Outside, the feared, the alien,
Hungry and dangerous.
His seed and Eve's fruit
At hazard from her rage.

Good wives wear amulets
Against her, to protect themselves.
Lilith is jealous.

God's Language

Angels have no memory,
God's language no grammar.
He speaks continually,
All words variations
Of his name, the world a web
Of names, each consonant
Proclaims a further meaning;
The unacceptable
Also the true, beyond
Time's bondage. Thus angels
Forget all contradictions,
Accepting every statement
As a commentary.
Their purpose is to gaze
Upon God's works, and listen,
Until the day that he
Pronounce the name: Messiah.

My Grandparents

Museums serve as my grandparents' house.
They are my heritage – but Europe's spoils,
Curios from furthest isles,
Barely compensate the fact
That all were dead before I was alive.

Through these high, dust-free halls, where
Temperature, humidity, access,
Are regulated, I walk at ease.
It is my family's house, and I
Safe and protected as a favoured child.

Variety does not exhaust me.
Each object witness to its own
Survival. The work endures beyond
Its history. Such proof supports me.
I do not tire of family treasures.

Because no one remembers who they were,
Obscure existences of which I am
The final product, I merit
Exhibition here, the museum's prize,
Memorial to their legend.

Vertical

Who told me my place?
 It takes generations
To breed such a true believer,
Centuries to produce
Someone who instinctively knew
The only movement possible
Was up or down. No space
For me on the earth's surface:
Horizontal equates with delusive
When only the vertical
Remains open to my use. But
I am released by language,
I escape through speech:
Which has no dimensions,
Demands no local habitation
Or allegiance, which sets me free
From whomsoever's definition:
Jew. Woman. Poet.

The Fall

Once you start falling, you fall forever.
Once you let go, there's no hold anywhere.
Wherever your home was, having left it
There can be no other. As a meteor,
Brightness increasing with velocity,
Hurtling through space, need never intersect
Any planet's orbit, you will not find
A resting place – nor end your journeying
until you've used up everything, consumed
Whatever feeds itself to you, is drawn
Into the plunging vortex of your fall:
Dark path you hope will lead furthest of all.

The Hebrew Sibyl

I who was driven mad and cast out
from the high walls of Syrian Babylon
I who announced the fire of God's anger
who prophesy to those about to die
divine riddles
am still God's oracle.

Mortals in Hellas will claim me
name me as from another city of birth –
Erythrae – one of the shameless.
Others will say I had an unknown father
and my mother was Circe
brand me a crazy impostor.

But when all has taken place
when the walls collapse and the Tower crumbles –
that coming time, when knowledge is lost
and men no longer understand each other –
no one will call me insane
but God's great sibyl.

Outside The Mansion

As though we stood with noses pressed against the glass
of a windowpane, outside a mansion, dazzled
by the glowing lamps, the music and the circling dancers:

festivity, ceremony, celebration,
all equally alien to my sort of person.
Such a failing passes down the generations.

It could well be a fairy story, half-remembered.
I've often wondered if some godmother uninvited
to the party, vengeful, cast her mournful spell.

So profoundly known, the joyless spite spoilers
use to ease such pain; envy and disappointment
proudly claim choice of the unavoidable.

Stronger than the doubt of being right or wrong,
that denial is our sole tradition. We watch
the windows darken as the curtains slide across.

Archive Film Material

At first it seemed a bank of swaying flowers
windblown beside a railway track, but then
I saw it was the turning heads of men
unloaded from the cattle trucks at Auschwitz.

Flies

November sun as warm as a Levantine
winter made me push my window up
this morning, brought back donkey-drivers' calls,
the look and smell of bakers' stalls and offal
butchers. (Flies were everywhere.)

But the shudder of glass (fear a splintering shard
might pierce me) from the frame carelessly jammed askew,
as heavy lorries brake and lower gear
to take the corner for a shortcut to the A40,
changed those images to Home County:
a pan of clarifying sugar syrup
on the Aga wrinkling as it starts to boil
(the crab-apple jelly-bag dripping draws flies
to the kitchen), or the irritable twitch
of a horse's flank to shift the biting flies.

The noise I heard could have been
the drone of a distant combine harvester,
a helicopter spraying, or closer still,
here in town, a treadle-machine next door
(that new family must be tailors) and their
muffled hullabaloo through the party wall (they're
killing each other: the flies are driving them crazy).

So I went to put the window down, to stop
the thrumming and its associations, and found
summer's last fly, trapped by the double-glazing.

Keeper

Mother's fur coats,
silver teapot and velvet
boxes of broken earrings.

Aunt Ann's crackle-glass lamp
with its patterned parchment shade,
her mahogany bookcase.

Daddy's volumes of Jewish Thoughts,
A Hermit in the Himalayas,
those plaid plus-fours.

A faded suitcase, corded,
the sort a schoolboy uses,
full of Harry's notebooks.

Albums of glossy photos.
The last smile dimmed,
since I heard about Cousin Fanny.

I see the family face
break through the surface
of Grandpa's speckled mirror

and hardly recognise myself.
Every object
claims me as its keeper,

souvenirs of joy
and anger I'm not sure whether
I want to cherish or destroy.

The Coptic Wedding

Decades go by, yet I keep mouthing
the same stupid lines.
I notice a bird in the park and can't
remember its name,
but wonder again, for the umpteenth time.

Young women behave
as if they have been taught to believe
a show of ignorance
charms every admirer. From someone
my age, that's tedious.

Where lay the harm
in my mother's reiterations
and nervous denials,
except to herself? My impatience
when she insisted
she'd never been there, heard of or done it –
whatever was mentioned –
like a child who always gets blamed,
still makes me ashamed.
She seemed afraid of everything.

Being stupid – or becoming like her –
was my worst fear
as a girl. When I forget, now,
what something's called,
it can conjure her up from the ground.

Celebration noise,
ululation and the throb of drumming
across the formal paths
and flowerbeds, drew every Sunday-
morning stroller
toward its source: a Coptic wedding,
a dancing circle
of white-robed men and henna-footed girls
around a couple
with solemn faces topped by golden crowns.

Our hunger for ceremony matched;
side by side we watched.
Neither of us would rest until
old promises were kept,
neglected rituals performed.

Far from her own ancestors
was how she must have felt, uprooted
as that groom and bride.
Recognising a chaffinch, I knew it.
All of us spun out of orbit.

Lineage

When my eyes were sore or tired or itched,
clenching her hand in a loose fist,
my mother would rub her wedding ring,
carefully, along the closed lids,
sure the touch of gold was curative.

She also believed in hot water
with lemon, first thing in the morning
and, at any time of day, drank awful-
tasting infusions and pot-liquors
to purify her blood. She warmed
a spoonful of sweet almond oil to pour
into my aching ear, wrapped torn
old woollen vests around my throat,
and blistered my chest with a poultice
if I came down with a cold.

Remedies and simples from the old
country, still useful in the city,
were passed from mother to daughter
and not yet scorned. We rarely saw
a doctor. When I was little
it seemed normal to be sickly
for half of the year. I never told her
that I was proud she was a witch.

Nature

'It's natural,' my mother would say,
as though the word had power to justify
and was the highest praise.
'Natural!' I scoffed. 'Like a cancer eating up someone.
Like war and death and pain.'

Nature meant flowers and babies
to her, not a slaughterer but a shepherdess.
She wouldn't have been out of place
at the Petit Trianon, with Marie Antoinette.
Remembering her panic-struck face

when I protested against
such Panglossian blindness to the indifference
of Nature, God, Fate –
whatever one called it (I was so infantile) –
still makes me itch with shame.

A girl of my age
should have known better, stopped tormenting her mother.
But when she went on about Nature
I refused to listen. She admitted nothing.
Not even gas chambers.

Horns

(This refers to the old belief that, as in Michelangelo's 'Moses', Jews are horned.)

Before my walk
I went to look
at the trusting calves,
their onyx eyes.
Instead, I saw,
livid, red,
between whorled hairs
white and black,
raw shallow wounds
and bloody clots
where budding horns
had been cauterised.

Then full recall –
the school playground:
its asphalt surface
gritty, harsh,
to knees and hands
of the one downed
by a press of children
daring each other
to push thick fingers
through springy curls
above her temples
and find the horns.

Elaine Feinstein

Buying a House for Now

To live here, grace
fills me like sunshine
these tall rooms

we walk through
singing: look
we have put down

a piano takes three men
to move, and
now sweeping

the pinewood floor
my mind is light
as blown glass

knowing to love what
can't be carried
is reckless

I testify
to the beauties
of now only

Song of Power

For the baiting
children in my
son's school class who
say I am a witch:
black is the
mirror you gave me.

Drawn inward at siege
sightless, mumbling:
criminal, to bear three
children like fruit
cannot be guarded
against enemies.

Should I have lived sterile?
The word returns me.
If any supernatural power
my strangeness earns me
I now invoke, for
all Gods are

anarchic even the Jews'
outside his own laws, with
his old name
confirms me, and I
call out for the
strange ones with wild hair

all the earth over to
make their own coherence,
a fire their children
may learn to bear at last
and not burn in.

Against Winter

His kiss a bristling
beard in my ear, at 83:
'aren't you afraid of
dying?' I asked him (on his knee).
who shall excell his shrug for answer?

and yet was it long after,
senile, he lived in our front room,
once I had to
hold a potty out for him, his
penis was pink and clean as a child

and what he remembered of
Odessa and the Europe he walked through
was gone like the language I
never learned to speak, that
gave him resistance,

and his own sense of
favour   (failed
rabbi, carpenter,
farmer in
Montreal)

and now I think
how the smell of
peppermint in his yellow
handkerchieves and the
snuff marks under his nose

were another part of it:
his sloven grace
(stronger than abstinence) that
was the source of his
undisciplined stamina.

Exile

Estonian ghosts of
river birds within the
temples of his skull, ashes
of poets, girders of school houses:
these are the tired politics
that vein his eyes

scoop a pouch under his lower
lip. In our system
his vigour has aged into
rumours of miraculous
sexual prowess, yet
the gesture of his
pasty fist is continuous with
the sag of his cardigan

and his enemies are
quiet middle-aged men, who
move in the mist of invisible
English power. He is
unhunted and unforested in the fen:
like the rest of us.

Bonds

There are owls in the garden and a dog barking.
After so many fevers and such loss,
I am holding you in my arms tonight, as if
your whole story were happening at once:
the eager child in lonely evacuation
waking into intelligence and then
manhood when we were first *copains*,
setting up tent in a rainy Cornish field, or
hitchhiking down to Marseilles together.

You were braver than I was and so
at your side I was never afraid, looking for
Dom 99 in the snows of suburban Moscow,
or carrying letters through Hungarian customs,
I learnt to trust your intuitions more than my own,
because you could meet Nobel laureates,
tramps and smugglers with the same confidence,
and your hunches worked, those molecular puzzles,
that filled the house with clay and wire models.

In the bad times, when like poor Tom Bowling,
you felt yourself gone for ever more,
and threw away all you deserved, you asked me
What was it all for? And I had no answer, then
or a long time after all that madness;
nor can I now suggest new happiness,
or hope of good fortune, other than
staying alive. But I know that lying at your side
I could enter the dark bed of silence like a bride.

Prayer for My Son

Most things I worry over never happen,
but this, disguised as an embarrassment,
turned risky in a day. Two years ago,
from the furthest edge of a blue sky,
an illness snatched his livelihood away.

Justice, Lord? How is this just? I
muttered, as if every generation must
learn the lesson again: there is
no special privilege protecting us.
He lay across his futon, white and thin

– the QEH sold out, his dep chosen –
in double torment. No one could comfort him.
I would have kissed the feet
of any holy man – as the Shunamite
woman did – to have the Lord relent.

But what since the miracle of his recovery?
Petty angers like a girlish sulk. Forgive
me such ingratitude. Let him only live
with grace, unthreatened, on the sound of his flute
– and I'll stop clamouring for sweeter fruit.

Waiting

The house is sick. When I come down
at night to the broken kitchen, the open wall, and find
a grey-haired and courteous old
cat asleep in a design of gypsum on the ground
I sense between iron girders and old
gas-pipes how many more ill-lit creatures of a damp
garden are waiting. Under the provisional blossom
of a plum tree they threaten a long siege
whispering: they shall eat sorrow
which is the flesh of the rat, the
dead limb in the locked room.
And I can hardly remember the dream of sunlight and
hot sweet wall-flowers that led us to break through
to the almost forgotten lord of the dark outside
whose spectres are part of his word, and whose promise of
home always demands the willingness to move on, who
forces me to acknowledge his ancient sign.

Some Thoughts on Where

For lovely Allen / I saw you dancing
on the telly last night: a black lion

you were lifting a monk's robe over
legs and feet at their bony male angles

smiling unforced unblown / high
over the seas that telstar moves on

you were beamed to us and we
in our local bother of where

we belong and how to   take your
airy scaling of skies as a sign

of what in the landscape of cities
has to be prized / mythic

nomad,   you live where you are   in
the now   the world you recognise is whirled in.

84

New Sadness / Old City

I saw Jerusalem from the Magog hills last night in
hot air the sky shaking:
white dust and crumbling stone and
the scent of scrubby hills

                    waterless
fort   Kohelech sadly and the
Egyptian before him whispers it
the death song of triumph   the desert
powders every man's eyelashes and
his cropped hair
                 gentle city, will
the saints of the Lublin ghetto
enter your streets invisibly and
marvel at last   or fear to

as we listened like ghosts
in a parked car here breathless when
you were taken   tasting on
our teeth uneasily the strange
illicit salts of elation.

The Celebrants*

VI

The red giant Antares is in Scorpio;
   in fen fields a radio dish listens.
Who will give us a horoscope for the planet?
   On December 3 which is the Day of the Emigrant,

for those who come of the ancient tribe of Habiru,
   nomads, wilderness people, having no
house of their own, or magicians; my desert
   grandmother laughed at the time to come.

Since then her daughters have seen Babylon
   Persepolis, Delphi, settled in Toledo
risen, and been flung over
   the north coast of Africa as Marranos.

From Clermont, the hill of the first Crusade
   we learnt things could be good only so long.
Our poets wrote that halls in heaven opened
   only to the voice of song, but their

boldest praise was always for
   the holy stamina of body and spirit as one
which is the only sacrament will stand to
   cold, fatigue, waiting, and starvation.

*This poem is taken from a nine-part sequence.

86

Green

In the resonance of that
lizard colour, mottled like stone from
Eilat with blue fruit and patches
of mud in it, my thoughts scatter

over Europe where there is water
and sunlight in collision, and green is
the flesh of Holbein's coffined Christ, and
also the liturgical colour of heaven.

In England: green is innocent as grass.

Dad

Your old hat hurts me, and those black
   fat raisins you liked to press into
my palm from your soft heavy hand.
   I see you staggering back up the path
with sacks of potatoes from some local farm,
   fresh eggs, flowers. Every day I grieve

for your great heart broken and you gone.
   You loved to watch the trees. This year
you did not see their Spring.
   The sky was freezing over the fen
as on that somewhere secretly appointed day
   you beached: cold, white-faced, shivering.

What happened, old bull, my loyal
   hoarse-voiced warrior? The hammer
blow that stopped you in your track
   and brought you to a hospital monitor
could not destroy your courage
   to the end you were
uncowed and unconcerned with pleasing anyone.

I think of you now as once again safely
   at my mother's side, the earth as
chosen as a bed, and feel most sorrow for
   all that was gentle in
my childhood buried there
   already forfeit, now forever lost.

Remembering Brecht

*'The man who laughs has not yet heard
the appalling news'*

That April, even though the trees were grey
    with something more than winter, when
I heard your voice and felt the first tremor
    of recovery, my joy was most mistaken,

which is not to say that living clenched with terror
    offers any protection. Other surprises
wait upon tears. Whatever we devise
    things may get worse.

Don't cry.   They often do.

Rose

Your pantry stocked with sweet cooked fish,
    pink herring, Polish cucumbers
in newspaper, and on the gas
    a bristly hen still boiling into soup:
most gentle sloven, how I honour now
    all your enormous, unfastidious welcome.

And when the string of two brown carrier bags
    bit into your short fat fingers
you only muttered, doesn't matter
    doesn't matter. I didn't understand
why you continued living with a man
    who could not forgive you, could not

forgive your worst offence:
    your happiness in little.
Even a string of shells would give you pleasure,
    but we did not bring gifts often;
and now it is too late to thank you for
    the warmth of your wide bosom, and the dimpled arms
waiting to hug my own bewildered children.

The Old Tailor

Yellow and bitter even
when we first met, I remember
   lenses already thick and insectivorous,
turning upon me their
   suspicious glare.

Your legend was familiar to me:
the sourlipped snarls your
   plucky wife smiled through,
the harshest sneers for
   anyone rash enough to take you on.

I wonder, now, how miserable you were,
   a clever child at school,
forced out to work. When did you first put on
   that brutal mask of blind
ferocity to hide the lonely certainty of failure?

New Year

Blue velvet, white satin, bone horn, once again
we are summoned today to consider mistakes and failures
into the shabby synagogue on Thompson's Lane.
Shopkeepers, scholars, children and middle-aged strangers
are gathering to mumble the ancient prayers,

because this is Rosh Hashonah, the New Year,
we have all come in out of the Cambridge streets
to look around and recognise the faces
of friends we almost think of as relations
and lost relations who never lived anywhere near.

How are we Jewish, and what brings us together
in this most puritan of Protestant centres?
Are the others talking to God, or do they remember
filial duties, or are they puzzled
themselves at the nature of being displaced?

I sit and think of the love between brothers,
my sons, who never took to festivals
happily seated round a family table;
I remember their laughter rising up to my bedroom,
late at night, playing music and cards together.

And as I look back on too many surprises
and face up to next year's uncertainties,
somehow I find it easier and easier
to pray. And this September, hope at least for
perfumes rising from a scrubby hedge
if not from flowering Birds of Paradise.

Annus Mirabilis 1989

Ten years ago, beneath the Hotel Astoria,
  we watched a dissident cabaret in Budapest,
where they showed Einstein as a Jewish tailor.
  All the women on stage were elegantly dressed.

Their silken garments were cleverly slit to expose
  illicit glimpses of delicate thighs and breast.
Einstein was covered with chalk, in ill-fitting clothes;
  he was taking measurements, trying to please the rest.

At the climax of the play, to applause and laughter
  they raked him with strobe lights and the noise of guns.
I was chilled by the audience euphoria.
  Of course, I don't have a word of Hungarian,

and afterwards there were embarrassed explanations,
  which left out tailoring and obsequious gestures.
Their indignation was all about nuclear science, while
  I pondered the resilience of an old monster.

Homecoming

The light is sullen today, yet people are
bustling in the rainy street under my window,

poking in the Cypriot grocers for aubergines,
buying their strings of garlic and onions;

they can choose between the many seeds on
the bread: rye, sesame, cumin.

Across the road, the pharmacy windows
are lettered in brass like a Victorian shop.

In the coffee house with its heavy green and gold
pottery, they serve bean soup with sausages

and the accents of old Vienna mingle
with California. In the countryside

every one of us would be found peculiar.
We'd leak away. In Englands Lane

(through road for taxis and the Camden hoppa)
this city music and a few friends keep me sane.

Amy Levy

Precocious, gifted girl, my nineteenth-century
voice of Xanthippe, I dreamed of you last night,
walking by the willows behind the Wren
and singing to me of Cambridge and unhappiness.

'Listen, I am the first of my kind, and
not without friends or recognition,
but my name belongs with my family
in Bayswater, where the ghosts

of wealthy Sephardim line the walls,
and there I am alien because I sing.
Here, it is my name that makes me strange.
A hundred years on, is it still the same?'

Allegiance

We like to eat looking at boats. At night
in Jaffa harbour, the whole sea is alight
with glow worms of the local fishermen's floats.

My English friend has blue flirtatious eyes
and feels no danger. Her intrepid forbears
first explored, then colonised the planet.

Now over Yemenite eggplant and fried dough
we talk about the Roman exploitation
of Caesarea two thousand years ago

and find the history easy to agree.
Politics here and now are another matter.
The scared, open faces of the soldiers

look like oppressors to her, while my inheritance
– Kovno, Odessa, packing and running away –
make me fear for them, as if they were sons.

So I can't share the privilege of guilt. Nor could
she taste the Hebrew of Adam in
the red earth here: the iron, salt and blood.

Prayer

The windows are black tonight. The lamp
at my bedside peering with its yellow
40 watt light can hardly make out the chair.
Nothing is stranger than the habit of prayer.

The face of God as seen on this planet
is rarely gentle: the young gazelle is food
for the predator; filmy shapes
that need little more than carbon and water,

evolve like patterns on Dawkins'
computer; the intricate miracles
of eye and wing respond to the same
logic. I accept the evidence.

God is the wish to live. Everywhere,
as carnivores lick their young with
tenderness, in the human struggle
nothing is stranger than the habit of prayer.

Karen Gershon

The Children's Exodus

I
It was an ordinary train
travelling across Germany
which gathered and took us away
those who saw us may have thought
that it was for a holiday
not being exiled being taught
to hate what we had loved in vain
brought us lasting injury

II
Our parents let us go
knowing that who stayed must die
but kept the truth from us although
they gave us to reality
did they consider what it meant
to become orphaned and not know
to be emotionally freed
when our childhood seeds were spent

III
When we went out of Germany
carrying six million lives
that was Jewish history
but each child was one refugee
we unlike the Egyptian slaves
were exiled individually
and each in desolation has
created his own wilderness

IV
This race-hatred was personal
we were condemned for what we were
no one escaped the ritual
from which we rose inferior
the blood-guilt entered every home
till daily life was a pogrom
we who were there are not the same
as those who have no wreck to share

V
Home is where some know who you are
the rescue was impersonal
it was no one's concern what use
we made of the years given us
one should not ask of children who
find their survival natural
gratitude for being where
ten thousand others have come too

VI
At Dovercourt the winter sea
was like God's mercy vast and wild
a fever to a land-locked child
it seemed fire and cloud to me
the world's blood and my blood were cold
the exiled Jew in me was old
and thoughts of death appalled me less
than knowledge of my loneliness

VII

My mother sold my bed and chair
while I expected to return
yet she had kept me close to her
till I saw our temple burn
it was not for her sake but mine
she knew that I was unripe fruit
and that exile was a blight
against which one prepared in vain

VIII

People at Dovercourt were gay
as if they thought we could forget
our homes in alien play
as if we were not German Jews
but mealtimes were a market place
when sudden visitors could choose
although we were not orphaned yet
a son or daughter by their face

IX

My childhood smoulders in the name
of the town which was my home
all we were became no more
than answers on a questionnaire
at Dovercourt we were taught that
our share of the Jewish fate
had not been left behind but was
the refugee life facing us

Home

The people have got used to her
they have watched her children grow
and behave as if she were
one of them – how can they know
that every time she leaves her home
she is terrified of them
that as a German Jew she sees
them as potential enemies

Because she knows what has been done
to children who were like her own
she cannot think their future safe
her parents must have felt at home
where none cared what became of them
and as a child she must have played
with people who in later life
would have killed her had she stayed

Generations*

The Male Line

IV
My grandson, like the almond tree,
blossoms in inclement weather.
With a runaway for a father
(without the parents of his father)
what shall he do for family?

Michael, milk the circumstances,
a tree grows stronger for standing alone.
With no footsteps to follow, pioneer.
The dyes of generations are
stored in the roots of your seedling senses:
proof that you are not on your own.

*This poem is from a six-part seequence.

103

Foster-England

The Land

Feeling closer to
the long-dead savages
from whose traces grow
ancestral images
than to the living men
with their 'how-do-you-do'
who lock their faces
against one like me,
I wish that I had come
in that century
when the mingling of races
made this their home.

The Language

Silent in Babylon
my sad fathers
laid my inheritance
on the flowing waters,
like the seed in the flesh,
word within anguish,
to grant me speech
in an alien language.

The Boy

A London boy caught
in his grey estate
skating down thoughts
to reach escape
with all green England
for his wage
and the cold sea tempered
in his look
and a swagger in
his Viking hair
took me to share
his anchorage.

Prognosis

I
Part of my future I know:
arthritis will cripple my hands,
my spine if I live to grow old;
to admit it is not the same
as having been told.

What frightens me has a name.

Such knowledge we share in vain,
within my skin I am alone.

II
The burning child I was
remains unreconciled
to making do with less
than once seemed possible:
no relationship whole,
no poem saying enough,
nothing as I imagined it,
all life at the mercy of
being randomly spoiled;
with my crooked fingers I write:
I am not reconciled.

III
I don't know what it's like for them,
it's an experience I lack;
my adult children coming home
have feelings I have never had:
when I was their age my parents were dead.

IV

Part of my future is plain:
I shall grow dependent on others;
what is it like for children
to have to look after their mothers?
And what might make my family
decide to let strangers look after me?
Will anything I do or don't do
make them make strangers look after me?

V

Suddenly they are everywhere,
old women who need looking after,
publicly chewing the cud of their troubles.
(Old woman, what is it like for you
to have become your daughter's child?)
She was never like me and I won't grow like her.
(Why does the street beset me with mirrors?)
When I am her age I'll not be as old.
(All around me potential doubles.)
I'll not let one of my daughters become
servant to an old woman like them.

VI

When I was their age and alone,
without family, without home,
my childhood harvested like corn
stored away and I unfed,
when no one cared what became of me,
I learned to care about others instead;
yet long after my first children were born,
when asked about my family
I would answer, they are dead.

VII
For twenty-eight years I have woven
my children's lives and mine
into a cunning tapestry
each has for his own;
it has a shifting centre
time must take me from.

Michael Hamburger

Judas Iscariot

No part was harder than his and none more cruel:
To be God's chosen villain in the absolute play,
Cast out by friends and enemies, cast out of self,
Hated by all for ever, hating himself;
And that the sinuous prophecy might be fulfilled,
Wriggle, a viper, down the appointed path,
Dust on his tongue,
Till he was dry and twisted as the final rope.

Pilate could speak of duty, Peter of human fear
Keener than love; but Judas could not speak,
For he had ripped out fear with the roots of love
And his inhuman duty was unspeakable.
Dust in his heart,
The inmost source of language clogged with dust,
He dreamed of sleep,
How in the end one drowsy snake would meet another,
Coiled in a dumb, yet passionate embrace.

That was the second kiss;
The first – how long ago it seemed – had killed him.
Might not the second give him life again?
Myopic men would hate him – so the play demanded –
But would the Master who gazed with different eyes?
A maze, a mystery was justice; only this he knew:
In God's own forge he had been melted down,
By God's own hammer beaten into murderous shape,
Betrayed into betraying.
After the deed, might not the instrument rest?

Or could it be that when the curtain fell on the last scene,
When, silent, the spectators stumbled home,
Still the actors were not dismissed, but in the dark
Must re-enact their parts?
If it was true that shroud and sepulchre could not contain
The Master's fiery spirit,
Then he for ever too, as Christ was Christ,
For ever must be Judas
And in a hell of cold self-hatred bite his tail.

Sleep, then, would be no refuge: never would he shed
His dark imprisoning skin, the dust of that long day,
Nor ever in the sweet still water bathe.

Reversal

From their source how easily
Dark artesian sorrows rise
And more like pleasures play
Transfused with daylight in her eyes.

Ah, but I told her so:
Now reversed those fountains race
From her dry but sullen face,
Daylight even sucked below.

A Horse's Eye

I did not stop today at the five-barred gate,
Did not wait for the old white draught-horse at grass,
Unshod, unharnessed these many years; walked past,
Preoccupied, but something made me look back:
Her head was over the gate, her neck was straight,
But I caught her eye, a wicked, reproachful look
From one small eye slanted in my direction.
What right, I defied the old mare, what right had she
To expect caresses, the grass foolishly plucked
For her hanging lip, her yellow, broken teeth
And her great historical belly? Of course she's a relic,
Curious now as the old white country house
That stood empty and alluring in the wood behind her
Till converted into flats not as useless as she,
Who will never become a tractor! What farmer would care?
Only some town-bred, animist, anthropomorphic rambler
Or week-end motorist looking for what he's lost.

I walked on; but plainly her glance had spoken to me,
As an old peasant's might in a foreign country,
Communicating neither words nor thought, but the
    knowledge
Of flesh that has suffered labour in rain and wind,
Fed, relaxed, enjoyed and opposed every season.
Broken now. Close to death. And how differently broken
From that Cossack mare the clumsiest rider could sit,
All speed and nerve and power that somehow responded
To the faintest twitch of a will less tense than her own!
Wild nature still; her eye no peasant's eye,
But lava under glass, tellurian fire contained.

As for the old white mare, her reproach was just:
Because she was too intelligible I had passed her by,
Because not alien enough, but broken as men are broken,
Because the old white house was converted now,
The wood about to be felled, a tractor chugging
Beyond the hill, and awkwardly she trotted
On legs too thin for her belly bloated with age,
Alone in her meadow, at grass, and close to death.

Blind Man

He can hear the owl's flight in daylight
When, surprised, on silky wings it shoots
From a low perch; and by the open window at night
The stag-beetles blundering in the hedges
On the far side of the meadow. Geese half a mile away
Honk near as hooters of swerving cars
And do not alarm him. Indifferently he awaits
Dogs that he feared when they slunk or bounded
Visible at him, as if in his carapace
Of darkness for ever secure from harm,
Wombed and housed and coffined within a wound
That has hardened to armour. The screech and the hum
Blend and subside in a resonant quiet,
Shapes he has fumbled to feel fall back
Into unbroken space when his hands forget them,
And still are present in his no man's land;
Above the nightmare tamed by light's extinction
The apple that hangs unplucked, grown fabulous.

Old Woman

She seems to drift, but talks against the current,
Observes a daffodil on the present bank
But strains toward its double of another spring
Not truly seen when seeing was too easy,
Her will less flexed against the drowsiness
Of dragging limbs, so near now to the sea,
With all the weight of eighty-six years to keep
From sleep that would be drowning.
So late she dare not drift, her work unfinished
As when a servant girl denied her sleep
To show the guests out, clear the table, polish
The silver cutlery, she dared not rest
Till almost night and morning drudgery met,
The silence was perfection.
And even now it's tidying keeps her up –
To talk her dead alive, sharp-tongued, cut through
Crust after crust of dirty circumstance
To set one legend free –
His whom by self-negation she upheld
Till the cold killers drove him from her tending
And out of memory,
Beyond her ken and kinship, wrenched his face.
Round, round she seems to whirl; but making, mending,
Laboriously retraces
A broken circle, his blurred lineaments;
Laughs as he laughed, and curses as he cursed
That she may come at last to where his voice gave out
Too soon, in the absurdity of death,
Smile as he smiled there, but less bitterly,
And, her work done, be still.

Security

1

So he's got there at last, been received as a partner –
In a firm going bankrupt;
Found the right place (walled garden), arranged for a
   mortgage –
But they're pulling the house down
To make room for traffic.

Worse winds are rising. He takes out new policies
For his furniture, for his life,
At a higher premium
Against more limited risks.

2

Who can face the winds, till the panes crack in their frames?
And if a man faced them, what in the end could he do
But look for shelter like all the rest?
The winds too are afraid, and blow from fear.

3

I hear my children at play
And recall that one branch of the elm-tree looks dead;
Also that twenty years ago now I could have been parchment
Cured and stretched for a lampshade,
Who now have children, a lampshade
And the fear of those winds.

I saw off the elm-tree branch
To find that the wood was sound;
Mend the fences yet again,
Knowing they'll keep out no one,
Let alone the winds.
For still my children play
And shall tomorrow, if the weather holds.

In A Cold Season

I
Words cannot reach him in his prison of words
Whose words killed men because those men were words
Women and children who to him were numbers
And still are numbers though reiterated
Launched into air to circle out of hearing
And drop unseen, their metal shells not broken.
Words cannot reach him though I spend more words
On words reporting words reiterated
When in his cage of words he answered words
That told how with his words he murdered men
Women and children who were words and numbers
And he remembered or could not remember
The words and numbers they reiterated
To trap in words the man who killed with words.
Words cannot reach the children, women, men
Who were not words or numbers till they died
Because ice-packed in terror shrunk minds clung
To numbers words that did not sob or whimper
As children do when packed in trucks to die
That did not die two deaths as mothers do
Who see their children packed in trucks to die.

II
Yet, Muse of the IN-trays, OUT-trays,
Shall he be left uncelebrated
For lack of resonant numbers calculated
To denote your hero, and our abstract age?
Rather in the appropriate vocabulary
Let a memorandum now be drawn up –
Carbon copies to all whom it may concern –
A monument in kind, a testimonial
To be filed for further reference
And to circulate as required.
Adolf Eichmann, civil servant (retired):
A mild man, meticulous in his ways,

As distinctly averse to violence
As to all other irregularities
Perpetrated in his presence,
Rudeness of speech or deportment,
Infringements of etiquette
Or downright incompetence, the gravest offence;
With a head for figures, a stable family life,
No abnormalities.

Never lost his temper on duty
Even with subordinates, even with elements earmarked
For liquidation;
Never once guilty of exceeding his authority
But careful always to confine his ambitions
Within the limits laid down for personnel of his grade.
Never, of course, a maker of policy,
But in its implementation at office level,
Down to the detailed directive, completely reliable;
Never, perhaps, indispensable,
Yet difficult to replace
Once he had mastered the formalities
Of his particular department
And familiarised himself with his responsibilities
As a specialist in the organisation
Of the transport and disposal of human material –
In short, an exemplary career.

III
Words words his words – and half his truth perhaps
If blinking, numb in moonlight and astray
A man can map the landmarks trace the shapes
That may be mountains icebergs or his tears
And he whose only zeal was to convert
Real women children men to words and numbers
Added to be subtracted leaving nothing
But aggregates and multiples of nothing
Can know what made him adept in not knowing
Feel what it was he could not would not feel –

And caged in words between their death his death
No place no time for memory to unfreeze
The single face that would belie his words
The single cry that proved his numbers wrong.

Probing his words with their words my words fail.
Cold cold with words I cannot break the shell
And almost dare not lest his whole truth be
To have no core but unreality.

IV

I heard no cry, nor saw her dying face,
Have never known the place, the day,
Whether by bullet, gas or deprivation
They finished her off who was old and ill enough
To die before long in her own good time;
Only that when they came to march her out of her human
world,
Creaking leather couch, mementoes, widow's urn,
They made her write a postcard to her son in England.
'Am going on a journey'; and that all those years
She had refused to travel even to save her life.
Too little I know of her life, her death,
Forget my last visit to her at the age of nine,
The goodbye like any other that was the last,
Only recall that she, mother of five, grandmother,
Freely could share with a child all her little realm;
Recall her lapdog who trembled and snapped up cheese –
Did they kill her lapdog also, or drive him away? –
And the bigger dog before that, a French bulldog, stuffed
To keep her company still after his early death.
Three goldfishes I recall, one with a hump on his back
That lived for years though daily she brushed her fishes
Under the kitchen tap to keep them healthy and clean;
And how she conspired with us children,
Bribed us with sweets if we promised not to tell
Our father that she, who was diabetic,
Kept a pillbox of sweets in her handbag

To eat like a child in secret –
When neither could guess that sweets would not cause her
    death.
A wireless set with earphones was part of the magic
She commanded and freely dispensed,
Being childlike herself and guileless and wise...

Too little I know of her wisdom, her life,
Only that, guileless, she died deprived
Of her lapdog even, stuffed bulldog and pillbox of sweets.

V
And yet and yet I would not have him die
Caged in his words their words – one deadly word
Setting the seal on unreality
Adding one number to the millions dead
Subtracting nothing from death dividing nothing
Silencing him who murdered words with words
Not one shell broken, not one word made flesh.
Nor in my hatred would imprison him
Who never free in fear and hatred served
Another's hatred which again was fear
So little life in him he dared not pity
Or if he pitied dared not act on pity;
But show him pity now for pity's sake
And for their sake who died for lack of pity;
Break from the husk at last one naked grain
That still may grow where the massed carrion lay
Bones piled on bones their only mourners bones
The inconceivable aggregate of the dead
Beyond all power to mourn or to avenge;
See man in him spare woman child in him
Though in the end he neither saw nor spared –
Peel off the husk for once and heed the grain,
Plant it though he sowed nothing poisoned growth;
Dare break one word and words may yet be whole.

The Road

It begins near Venice,
A Venice of chasms and pools,
And above a coastline longer than vision
Gently curves
Into a south or east without end.
Always the question is
How far can I walk it
Across what frontiers
Into what vastnesses,
More golden mist,
Woods ever denser, darker,
Mountains more mountainous
Above a more dazzling sea.

Always I am detained;
As by this new nation
Of displaced persons
Who are rarely visited,
Whose nationhood is a cause.
They needed me,
Appealed to my friendship,
Involved me in schemes,
Charged me with missions
To friends whom I never reached.

If only I could move on
To the wilder, more alien countries
Farther along the road.

The Search

As commanded, I looked for my origin,
Passed through the town in which my grandfather settled
And found no street that I knew;
On through the suburbs, blind bungalows,
Lilac, laburnum, narrowly flowering
And out into mountains, woods,
Far provinces, infinities of green.
Walked, walked, by day, by night,
Always sure of the route
Though the people grew foreign, bizarre;
And the birds, a species unheard of, remembered me.
At last I came to a village
Where they told me: here you were born.
An unlikely place – no petrol pump, office block, poster? –
Yet I could not deny it, and asked them the name.
Why, Mors, need we tell you, m o r s, MORS.

Woodland Lake
for E.B.

Parkland once, on the right bank of the Thames,
And the lake an artefact
Dug out of sodden clay to be wholly possessed
As the river could not be; now private beyond the design,
Moated with man-high nettles,
Scrub and bramble, ankle-deep mire, dead branches,
Fulfilled. Black crystal. Never so darkly limpid
When before leisure's decay
Keepers dredged it, a lady walking alone
In the scream of a peacock heard all her acres lies still.

Mottled with willow shade
Moorhen and mallard drift on nobody's water.
And higher, it seems, through boughs overhanging or
    mirrored,
Basking, languidly gliding,
Left behind, suspended, two golden carp,
Their bulk, their age immune, the lake's time theirs.

Dust

1

Living with it, till the flakes
Are thick enough to pick up
With my fingers and drop
Into waste paper basket, bin
Or bowl, whichever is nearest,
Must I recant, take back
My 'hymns to dusters' (unwritten)
Now that she they were meant for dusts
Another man's rooms? A traitor,
In turn, not to her but all
Those heroic housewives, charwomen,
Worldwide relentless army
Fighting the stuff with equipment
So various, intricate, fussy,
It scares me, as dust does not?
Dropped out, for good, from that unending campaign,
Their daily advance by inches,
Their nightly retreat by as many
Or more; the chemical warfare,
The cleaning of cleaning utensils,
Maintenance of the means of maintaining
What never can be maintained.

No, I'll revoke nothing,
Not even revoked love,
Things that dust blurs or dust
Blown away uncovers,
Awed, as before, by the valour
Of grappling till death with death;
But, tainted, feel free to prefer
The smell of dust to the smell
Of disinfectants, polish,
Floorcloth and mop, breathing in
Matter's light breath, exhalation
That mingles pollen with down,

Germs with ashes, and falls
On my brooms, my vacuum cleaner,
On the whiteness of pillow, paper,
Unendingly falls, whirls,
Drifts or settles, fertile
And deadly, like being alive.

2

And yet in a dream I see them,
The dreamers of reason, the cleaners
Humanly march to the coast
Of every ocean on earth
To clear the beaches, reform
Those flotsam-retching waters,
Their seaweed-killer guns
Cocked in the cause of order.
The music I hear, dreaming,
Is canon, fugue, ricercare,
No slop, no loose ends.
If they sing there, under
A cloudless sky, while they let
Pure sand run through their fingers,
The waves hold back, it is:
Veni creator spiritus,
Antibiotic, make us
More than the dust that we are.
Lest we lie too long in bed,
Daydreaming, of night,
Of nature's way with our flesh,
Come, spirit, and destroy
What merely lives and dies;
Give us the dream of reason.

I wake to the howling of winds.
To darkness. I breathe dust.

Weeding

1

Here I am again with my sickle, spade, hoe
To decide over life and death, presume to call
This plant a 'weed', that one a 'flower',
Adam's prerogative, hereditary power
I can't renounce. And yet I know, I know,
It is a single generator drives them all,
And drives my murderous, my ordering hand.

These foxgloves, these red poppies, I let them stand,
Though I did not sow them. Slash the fruit-bearing bramble,
Dig out ground elder, bindweed, stinging nettle,
Real rivals, invaders whose roots ramble,
Robbing or strangling those of more delicate plants.
Or perhaps it's their strength, putting me on my mettle
To fight them for space, resist their advance.

2

I stop. I drop the spade,
Mop my face, consider:
Who's overrun the earth
And almost outrun it?
Who'll make it run out?
Who bores and guts it,
Pollutes and mutates it,
Corrodes and explodes it?
Each leaf that I laid
On the soil will feed it,
Turning death into birth.
If the cycle is breaking
Who brought it about?

3

I shall go again to the overgrown plot
With my sickle, hoe, spade,
But no weedkiller, however selective,
No chemicals, no machine.
Already the nettles, ground elder, bindweed
Spring up again.
It's a good fight, as long as neither wins,
There are fruit to pick, unpoisoned,
Weeds to look at. I call them 'wild flowers'.

At Staufen
for Peter Huchel

1

'Too tame, too pretty', you said,
Sitting in front of your borrowed villa
Overlooking vineyards, the wide plain
That far off, when the haze lifts,
Outlines the Vosges;
Or, if you turned your head,
Closer, the mountainous fringe
Of the forest they call black.

Not black enough, for you,
Driven out of your true home,
The menaced, the menacing East?
Tamed for timber, tended,
Its nature trails
Pedagogically furnished
With the names and provenance
Of representative trees;
And the foxes gone,
Gassed, for fear of rabies.

Not black enough, for you,
On their hill, the castle ruins
Pedagogically preserved
With a plaque for Faust?

2

Yet the homeless cats,
Untouchable, gone wild,
Came to you for food,
One of them dragging
A leg ripped by shot.
Above the swimming pool
Buzzards hung, cried.
High up, from a treetop
An oriole slid
Through its small range of tones
And once, once only
Flashed in quick flight,
Making oak, ash, fir
Look blacker.

Nor would you let
Ladybirds, butterflies
Drown, or be gutted alive
By the black water beetle
That ruled the pool.

Too late I skimmed off
A golden gardener,
And returned to my book,
Old-fashioned Fabre's
'Social Life in the Insect World' –
To find that very species
Observed, recorded there:
Its mass killing
Of caterpillars,
The female's nuptial feast
On the male.

I closed the book,
And kept the corpse
For the green and gold of its wings.

3

Dark the gravestones were, too,
At Sulzburg, the Hebrew letters
Blacked out by centuries
Of moss on the oldest;
With no new ones to come,
With the last of a long line
Gassed, east of here, gone.

Well tended, fenced off
From the camping ground
And the forest's encroachment,
That site was black enough
Even where sunbeams lit
New leaves, white flowers.

You said nothing, looking:
Slabs of stone, lettered or blank,
Stuck into black loam.
The names that remained, German;
The later inscriptions, German;
No stone, no inscription
For the last of the line,
Who were carrion, Jewish.

4

Yes, much blacker they'll be,
Much bleaker, our landscapes,
before 'Desert is our history,
Termites with their pincers
Write it
On sand.'

But with eyes that long have stared
Into the dark, seeing,
You can look still
At the vineyards, the forest's edge
Where even now
A pine-marten kills, as it must,
Wild or tame prey;

Still can feed
The homeless cats,
Can save, as you must,
From natural, from
Man-made death
Insects that, brilliant or drab,
Are skilled, fulfilled in killing
And willing, in turn, to be killed;

Can write, still, write
For the killers, the savers
While they survive.
For the termites, eaters
Of paper, while they survive.
Or the sand alone,
For the blank sand.

Willow

Hard wood or soft?
It is light, startlingly,
Not close-grained, to last
As oak does; but makes up
In obstinate wiry toughness for that
With all its fibres.
From the barkless bough
My axe rebounds;
My handsaw bends,
From the sham death
Willow, by shamming, defies.

Pick any twig, dormant
Or wrenched off in a gale,
Stick it in moist earth,
And it makes a tree.
Leave a trunk, fallen
Or felled, sprawling
Across a stream,
And it lives on,
Sprouts from the hollow
Half-rotten stump or
Takes root from a dropped limb.

Chop up the dry remains,
Burn them: they'll spit.

Night...

Night. A man clears a border, throwing
Plucked weeds, broken-off twigs of shrubs
Forward, against the wall of his house, against
That in the air which whispers: so late, so late.
Delinquent hands. Delinquency of hands
Driven to impose an order still on rankness
When, our own order lost, we are less than grass.
Labours in drum-taut stillness, pauses, and hears
Mated shrieks of barn-owl and moorhen,
Vixen and leveret in the one dark's grip;
Knowing: lostness it is that keeps me, that holds me here.
Till another cry rips him, his own name
Called out again and again, in the house,
By her his absence has woken, who looks for him now,
Whom, so near, so near, he can summon no voice to answer,
No motion to comfort, his feet leaden with loss.

Winter Aconite, Adonis

Not ostentatious either, long before
The trumpeted daffodils
Make spring official, but so small
That one must know the patch, clear it of sodden grass
To see the curled stalks bear
Furled yellow into still forbidding air
Of this last January day,
Opening only when the sun gets through
Or never, should the drizzle and the mist
Forbiddingly persist.
Furled or unfurled, foreknown or unforeknown,
By sheer anachronism more they will surprise
Than snowdrop white that's wintry to our eyes;
And before snowdrops may have come and gone –

Unlike adonis, built to last, defy
All sorts of weather, by holding back
The sturdier blossom on the sturdier stalk
For weeks, or months if need be, cunningly,
Leafage wrapped round it, and a tinge of green
Outside the yellow petals, for disguise,
Unfurling, furling, till true warmth sets in.
Then let the fanfares blare,
The pampered pomp of frilly daffodils blaze!
Its work is done, in frost's and wind's despite,
To put on death now, sweet
While all and sundry feast on the easier air.

Migrants

Inside the house, betrayed by her heart and the bowels
That to her were indecent as death,
Lies the great-grandmother, brave and unwise till now
As robin, blackbird, bluetit alighting still
On her window-sill to be fed
With the biscuit crumbs that for once she can't rise to strew,
Chirpy always in poverty, widowhood
Until the tears all strange to her bird's eyes,
Human, welled up from a lifetime's forbidden darknesses.

Outside, we dare not report, on telephone wires
Martins and swallows have gathered,
Ready to leave, early this year.

Animula, spirit so little, so light
For so strenuous a flight to a place so far from the house.

Literary

A fellow scribbler shows me his latest poem,
Hands me the sheet
And the letters, too small to read with the naked eye,
Are moving indeed: mites
That crawl here and there, shifty,
One or two right over the edge of the paper.
Does it matter, I ask, if they disappear?
No, he says, there are others to take their places.

Through strong lenses I can follow
Their permutations, lively enough, suggestive,
Recoiling only when the more sinister kinds
Leave the page and threaten my skin.

Endless

It began as a couch grass root,
Stringy and white,
Straggling, to no end,
Branching out, breaking
For procreation.

Traced and pulled, it became
A bramble shoot that climbed
Through leafage of shrub, tree
With a root at its tip, for plunging.

I pulled at it, pulled,
Miles of the thing came away,
More and more.

I pulled and pulled until
I saw that now
Straight up it had risen
With its end in space,
With a root in heaven.

Homeless

In the garden grown mountainous, rocky
Some blight had settled on the trunk of a tree
That half stood, half lay.
I climbed it, to see:
Like sawdust out of a cloth doll
It had looked from a distance, but now
Was a hollow, a pool.
Inside it, a human body,
Not a corpse afloat,
A naked body, androgynous, ageless,
Immersed and alive.
At first I felt I must save it,
Drag it out, and looked for help
From my housemates below.
Then I knew it belonged there,
A being that breathed under water.

Suddenly there were deer,
Stag-sized, so fallen from shyness
That they would not move when I touched them,
Barred my way, took over.
Other animals walked or loitered
As though they had always lived here.
In vague haste I glimpsed them before
All the vistas, the empty spaces,
Openings into land or sky
Filled up, darkened
With a wave of brown particles
Compacted, as of sawdust
From sodden, rotten wood
That so fast, so widely surged in,
There was no more time for discerning,
Telling tame from wild, near from far,
The known from the unknown.

Three Miles From The Coast

Morning it must be, the nightly gale passed over
Whose moaning, whining had gnawed at our sleep.

Low still, at threshold level
Sea water laps the foundations.

At a first floor window I stand
Looking, wondering how the immersion will change
The garden two decades of labour made mine,
The trees I raised from seed or cutting or sucker
And the older ones tended, maintained.

As yet none lies uprooted
Though something white, roundish –
A buoy, a flimsy urn, mere flotsam? –
Bobs at the beech hedge's base.

How can I know that it is the sea
When rains and the river had flooded these parts before,
But feel no fear for the house, the village,
For my nearest, no impulse to save or flee?

Too far the water stretches, and quiet now
As the sky, as unshored, unbounded.

It is what comes and must come,
Was before living or dead beam had risen here
And overnight or more slowly must ebb again
From our, from others', from nobody's land.

Winter Solstice, 1999

Dream of the trees found in a dubious garden
Estranged by age and blight, a silver birch
Somehow I'd dragged there living from another,
Dug in too loosely, so that the thick trunk wobbled
Between new growth and atrophy of old roots;
But evergreen this holly recognized as the one
Raised from a first-year seedling, transplanted here.

Damp, dark and cold the dawn awakening,
All my dead in it, dubious as the trees,
No moonshine mixed into the grey of morning,
Silence before the foraging birds descend,
And no more mine in this light than in dream
The garden was that once I must have tended,
Than those will be whom in the street I pass
With sprigs of holly or yew, remembering words.

Day, year and century hang by a spider's thread.

Philip Hobsbaum

Testimony

She laughed, mocking herself, for the angel said
'I shall return when Sarah has a son'.
Ninety years' withering away could do
More than the word of God – so Sarah knew.

The laughter spread, it grew, that all might join
In her impossible joy as she suckled her child.
'Is any thing too hard for the Lord?
Are not miracles nature misconstrued,

Nature the constant miracle?' Once I
Joined hoarsely in the singing, as dogs do,
With inarticulate pain. Should I not rejoice
After these barren years being given a voice?

A Poem for my Daughter

I seem to see us going to the zoo,
You scampering, I pacing. Bears awake
Your laughter, apes your scorn, turtles your rage –
'Great floppy things,' you say, 'what can they do?'
You run off; and I bellow after you –
Brown legs flickering under short white frock –
Standing in impotent call while you glance back
Laughing, and run off laughing. I run, too,

And bump into a friend, grown middle aged,
Point out my curious daughter, paused to see,
Wave, make you come at last. You shyly wait
Finger in mouth, huge brown eyes wondering, I
Resting my hand on your curly dark head;
Knowing you are not, and may never be.

Man Without God: a sequence

I wake up spitting out of God knows what
Dark of writhing struggle and release
Mouth bitter with blood bitten where teeth
Into the soft red flesh of my cheek bit
Into its living pith in frenzy bit...
I climb slowly out of bed. The glass
Shows me a heavy and unshaven face
In some way changed, afflicted by the night.

I do not grimace, pain stiffens my cheek,
I dab out blood instead. It will heal,
That flesh; my tongue stops lightly over scars
Knitting the ravaged surface. But I look
To the unfamiliar contour of my jowl
Which seems a little thinner than it was.

'Playing the piano in gloves' bellowed out
The pub urinal gent close to my ear.
No doubt he thought of sex in sheaths; but I
Thought of our native claws grown blunt, our taste
Dainty, skins prettily wrapped; we need
Food killed discreetly where we won't smell blood,
Cleanly packaged, sliced up and passed out
Hygienically, so we can file and write

Insulated by steel and glass from storm,
Issuing out to walls of shops, sealed
Roads, even the sky veiled with soot.
One of our better bombs would take the roof
Clean off our lives – a few survivors might
Hew rock, heap leaves, bring supper dripping home.

In practice we forget the knife at our throat,
Sewers alive with death sealed away
Under our hurrying feet, the convenient car
Skidding on roads made slippery with our blood.

143

Mortality should intimate each flight
Of steps is, too, a fall – and each clear
Pane holds daggers in suspension, fire
Chars bone, stoves choke, and even light

Shocks to quiescence you who say these are all
Leashed in, damped down. A yard of kids at play
I walked; one lost a ball, another fell –
At once a groan deep and insatiate rose.
You'd blow your brains out whistling that away;
The knife had slipped, the mask dropped from the beast.

How they have baited through the tortuous years
Our souls with these unlikely tales. A man
Swallowed a fruit and damned us. Or a man
Was told to cut his own boy's throat. Wagers
Stripped another just to make him curse
And die. Another, fastened to a beam,
Died for us all, they say God's only son
Nailed up to please his father. Holy wars

Convinced the infidel of this. I'm not
A martyr, I'm afraid – I'd be convinced
As soon as they brought the tongs in. No one died
For me or settled sins upon my head
(Though I'm as oppressed with guilt as if they had)
And I live, I don't die when I curse God.

At times I feel so inside out you could
Show me a negative I'd see it clear.
I live my life just as I want and fear
No after-life, no ghost, no prayer, no God –
No need, you'd say, to fear death. Yet my God
I do! I need some shape for life – up there
An eye ought to be kept – someone should care
If only from his absence understood.

144

One wet night instead of the usual pub
I went to a place where people talked to God:
Men slaved to vault that roof, and a myth
Turned into truth as buttresses heaved up.
It isn't rage I feel at such men's faith
But wonder that they had what most I need.

Old gipsy woman swathed in shawls you bend
Shifting the candlesticks in muffled prayer
Not understood by anybody here
Except for God, perhaps. Not me, aged ten –
'Booba, why do you light these candles?' Flame
Begins to live, at last she turns to hear
Her grandchild. 'When they light these everywhere
M'shiach will come to lead us into Zion.'

Safe and aloof, from silver candlesticks,
A blue heart at each core, stream up the flames
As steady as my burning faith not hers
Which wavered when I heard her telling sums
Schnorrers borrowed in pence over the years:
'I'll get my money – when M'shiach comes!'

'O them angels! O I think I see them!'
'The sweat-streaked face splits to a cavernous O,
Body bends slowly back, arms rise up to
The single shaft of sunlight striking down
Into the smoke and stink of the ballroom,
Spilled drinks, torn flowers, mangled food, sad go
Round of slumping bodies shuffling. 'O –'
He cries still, black cross quartering a burst drum.

The one cool bystander suggests 'Heroin'.
So, they say, love is chemicals, and vision
Electrical impulses within the brain –
This does not make love lust or vision dream.
For visionaries things are what they seem:
The drummer embraces angels in the dawn.

145

When I was a child I lived in a great house
With stairs each a stride high, every room
Dangerous with discovery, broad floors strung
With wires, mirrors concealing plugs, reels hung
From chairs for cats to play with, double doors
Opening out to rolling hills of grass
And hollyhocks bobbing against the sun.
When my godlike parents struck me, I was wrong.

I've been back since to that narrow awkward house,
Stumbled down dark stairs to the living-room
Barricaded with furniture; the garden's
Scrubby with weeds. Old folk live there now,
Much like my parents. Twenty years ago
I wept to find them out. The shock remains.

If you made the right faces and muttered the right words
Your sums would come out right, Dad not be cross.
If you avoided the cracks in the pavement perhaps
You wouldn't, though late, be so. Such were my hopes,
My faith at ten! Sums tied themselves in knots
Only a smack could sever, the bell's sound
Clanked shut the moment I, puffing, came round
The corner. I still propitiated my gods.

Even puberty seemed (those years of care!)
To need more than adjustment. Late for a date
I'd curse the buses to make them come. And, sick,
I'd tussle with hopes, fears, even hopeless prayer
Wouldn't have seemed out of place. We thank God, well,
For making us well; but who first made us ill?

When the Shofar summoning the tribes
Turned into old men sucking asthmatically
At rams' horns, when deep-chested chants became
A gabbled gibberish, and my grandfather
Who'd made the day a Sabbath with his cane,
His top hat, frock coat, silver-streaming beard,
Dwindled to shrivelled hide and hair, then died –
God ebbed away, and could not be descried.

The need remains – the desperate search in friends
For what no human being could afford,
And sadness at betrayal; the drain out
Of life of all meaning – till the book you read
Is print, that picture paint, and even people
Are stilted things, horribly vertical.

The sky was darker than the reclining hills
Glimmering distantly, the murky air
Was filled with boys' shrill cries, the poplar trees
Stood out against the clouds, the ditch-like stream
Glugged muddily behind me, and the kids
Chasing a shadowy ball fell over, screamed,
Got up and chased again. Cold, with my whistle
Ready between my teeth, I stamped my feet,

Then down a shaft of sunlight struck the trees
Into tall flames – flames, they were, streaming up
Into a purple sky – then the grey grass
Streamed green around me, life, I saw, a flux
Pushing the flower out between the rocks,
Splitting to children racing under the clouds.

Bulldog Drummond Fights Again

Huge, often swathed in black, cheerily shouting
'Come on, boys' as you crash through the closed windows
Into the drawing-room packed full of crooks,

See how you seize two Chinese by their pigtails,
Smashing their yellow skulls together, then
Duck mysteriously a knife from behind.

'Not done to fight with knives,' you say, and so
You lash him to a chair, then with a whip
Chastise him till he weeps. Justice is done,

Is done, and done again. Caught on dark stairs
Arms of prodigious length around your throat
You slash an artery somewhere – that's all right,

The man's a chink or wop or wog or boche.
The jews are worst. 'What are these Hebrews here?'
(A henchman comes and whispers.) 'Is that so?'

Out comes the whip again. They squeal with fear,
Not unnaturally. *You* don't, of course –
Batter you into the mud, you'd come out singing.

And how you'd hate me! Intellectual Jew,
Reading books, disliking sport and games,
I couldn't join your club, you'd brain me with it.

You're an old has-been now, dust on your shelf.
Time was they'd crowd around the letter S
On the off chance of Sapper coming in.

We've other things to give our hate release.
The TV Marlowe, pulped and broken-toothed,
Peter Cushing torturing young girls,

And, of course, our own science fiction. We've a device
Would scorch you up worse than Carl Peterson.
Even you never filled the rain with death,

But your sons are trying hard. The bruisers' faces
Of young M.P.s, those puffy brigadiers,
Voices deceptively mild, assure us we

Can give the Enemy worse than he's got.
Who is the Enemy? They hardly care.
I read to numb my uttermost despair

Till Bulldog Drummonds us from off the earth.

The World's Great Hospital

Unthinking at first I noticed, propping up walls,
Dressing the doors of pubs, scattered over
The streets like so many waiting dummies, all
The warped children of some monstrous father.

Here a head blows out of a stalky frame,
There, trunk and hump burden a legless waist,
This moves only in a disastrous game,
One leg tucked up behind as he hops past –

God's chosen people! In a back alley, we've
A Cripple's Institute, and, after good works,
– For what can a cripple do, make baskets, weave? –
We let them out to take the air of the streets.

Passengers trundle along, bowl from the shops
Laden with packages. These marked men stand
Posted like sentinels wherever we cross,
Strangers and foreigners both in our own land.

The Neurotic

Sometimes I feel it creeping up on me,
Breathe on my stiff neck like a lecherous dog
Or, coiled around my feet, crash me down.
Days I sit waiting for it – here it comes,
Crick in the back, tic in the cheek, my nose
Slowly silting up. And in the evening
Bang! down it comes like a blanket over my head –
I have to get out, I have to drink all night,
Then come home, bland and baffled, glad to escape
Even at that expense, my gnawing mind.

I see the new-limned tracery in her face
And wonder how much's mine – the cobwebs form
About her eyes, and I, the artist, drew them.
At times the smallest thing she does grates
On my ear, scrapes the exposed raw nerve –
It's not that I don't love her, maybe I
Love my neurosis more. I hug it to me,
At night, insomniac, we stroll the streets
Grumbling together, then in the early dawn
Steal back like thieves to an uneasy bed.

There is this spring inside me that's wound up:
The smallest check can make it whip out sharp
And lash the innocent hand that's prodding me.
We all got slapped at school, or screwed our eyes
Unable to see the blackboard –I'm the kid
It's happening to at thirty. How do you cure
A wincing soul – a dog that fears the worst
Because the worst has happened too many times?
Cut off my frontal lobes, inject a cure,
Some smooth, some lovely allay to soothe me down,
Give me the confidence the snivelling child,
Unloved because unlovely, never had,
Make me not need the love I never got?

The Ice Skaters

They merrily weave over the blue transparency,
Fir trees against snow-threatening sky etched
Nicely in, curvet, chassée, and slide

Merrily off – a long take, this time. I see them
Shining blonde and lustrous dark and honey-
coloured meet, escape, pirouette, and off again

Over the smooth hard sheen. Under their legs
Twirling so merrily what deep acres live
Of dark or weed or slow fish nudging past,

What bottom-sods of mud, what tangles of weed –
They slide over the surface, beckoning us on,
Gingerly we follow, test the security – fine,

They call, weaving away merrily. You
Venture to catch them up, reach out, and
Find yourself struggling in dirty water. Call,

Ice in your mouth, spluttering blindly, down,
Down into the mud, entangling with weed you go.
Their laughter tinkles prettily over the ice.

Dream Children

I had this dream. We were all drinking together,
But I was watching the time – you had to go home,
All of you, out of the fug, into your beds
Clean and white, the healthy wakening, work.
So rang for a taxi, talked hard to get you in.
One said she'd stop for another, another had a friend
She ought to pick up, a third – well, that third got lost,
I searched like a maniac for her, forced in the rest.
We started. Oh, what a route! Up hilly streets,
Past derelict shops, blind windows, holes in the wall,
We rattled and groaned. What detours! 'Where are we now?'
I'd yell, peering through crusted glass to the night
Solidly banked beyond. We trundled still –
You chattered, she chattered, we stopped, we started – someone
Whoever it was, had a bottle. We drank some more:
I woke up sweating. Never, it seemed, would we
Find our way home, you lost in the night,
Boozing and sleeping around, I locked in my head,
Seeking and seeking for what I shall never have.

The Sick Lion

retreats to his hidden fastnesses to lick
his bleeding paws, blink vengefully at the gloom,
sullen and unconsoled. All night
the forest is shaken by profound complaints,
growling, reverberant. Lesser denizens
creep about twilight tasks assigned to fear,
hope unobtrusively. The other beasts
keep well away, scenting the sickness, leave
him to his waking pain. Until the day,
sinews sewn up, torn ligaments healed, he leaps
out in a blaze of thunder, tears the bush
clean from the earth, lays waste the pest of fowls,
jackals, camp-followers. That will be the day
when all find themselves judged for their detachment,
when the jungle, at last, assumes its rightful name.

Watching and Waiting

Why do I sit so chastely by your side
In this lone field, not tumble you, not slide
Ever so gently my hand up your bare thigh?
Because I live in hope. There is no doubt,
No doubt at all that one day your dear
Eyes will search into mine and find their peace.
Therefore I live in hope. The smallest touch,
Whiff of a shared cigarette, is more to me
Than nine years' broken marriage. I can wait,
Wait in the cold, in the dark, warm myself
At the flames of my hope. And should it come to pass
That this hope, too, proves futile, and in hell
I lie consumed with passion, even then,
As poets say the damned do, I will slake
My scorched eyes on that heaven divorced from me
And live, as now, in hope.

The Invisible Man

I stagger, buffeted by winds
Channelled between drizzling black crags –
Tenement buildings. Take refuge in a pub
Only to see in the mirror the bald streak widen,
Troubled by the blonde in the corner. Silly,
She doesn't know I'm here.
                    Strangers
Pause if I speak, resume their chat. As I go
I take this vacancy with me. The world outside
Drives its cars, pushes its prams. I'm air
In this too solid city.
                    Yet I pause
Buffeted by people buffeting past, stand
On this perpetual street corner of my life,
Look back. I am the abyss. And it claims me.

The Sick Monkey

will not be chosen by females of the tribe,
remains forever on outskirts, or you see him
feeding uneasily between two cadet males.
Maybe he shows his teeth too much, or hints
at latent aggression. That doesn't get him in.
Sometimes he lures aside some other male
and takes his food away. But that's no good,
the tribe will side with those that side with them –
willing to volunteer, patient with others,
kind to the young. Strength's not enough, it seems,
and so he lurks apart, casting his glance
at an inner circle he's not asked to join,
knowing in his childish monkey way
that apes can't use an ape-man, that the tribe
survives on compromises, give and take.
Yet knowing, too, he'd only to be trusted
to become most trustworthy, needing the love
a tribe affords to be, what he would be,
a decent lover, but guessing, in his way,
that only a holocaust could bring him out.

Messbaum Tells Some Jokes

'A poor, sick Jew' – James T. Farrell

1

'This is my handbag' she said 'nobody likes him,
He hangs around too many pubs getting old
And, frankly, rather shabby. Do you know
I think quite soon I'll have to pension him off.
His name is Basil.' I replied 'Call him Philip.'

2

I do not know where my friend and my girl are sleeping,
Most likely together, but I know where I'll sleep.
There is a place called the Slime Garden,
The worst place in the world,
Where only bottles and soaking papers grow
And slugs and worms.
Tonight I shall lie down among those worms
And tell them jokes like this. They have no faces,
So they must look at my face to make up.

3

I only drink in a bar that has a cellar.
That way
My friends can hear me howling from the abyss.

4

You always know, I told my girl, when
I really fancy you,
Green tentacles reach towards you out of my head.

158

5

If I were minus four feet high I could
Quite easily walk about under your feet.

6

You are a hammer? Smash me.
You are a fire? Burn me.
You are neurosis? Ride me.
You are my friend? Climb upon my back.

7

When I come on earth again I want to be
A camelephantelopelicanary.
I'd fit in anywhere.

8

It's fun being a schizophrenic.
At least you are never alone.

9

My nose is a little factory for producing grot.
My eyes are red-hot lumps of coke.
Each day I climb towards God on a river of shit.
He deserves it. I am, perhaps, his least funny joke.

'Professor Grottmann Explains Everything' (extract)

6

When my poor friend was in tears I comforted him, saying
'You wished all this misery on yourself
By putting us in this position.'
When he shrieked out denials I explained to him gently
That, in effect, it was all for his own good.
True, he was lying awake next door while I was ploughing her
But, since I explained to him in great detail our sex-play,
He cannot deny that I gave her more pleasure than he could
(Oh madam, I am a patient and successful lover).
And he cannot deny that I am, at least, a useful intermediary
Or half-way house.
And, indeed, in so far as he is a masochist,
He must have enjoyed being unhappy.
In any case I have no intention of marrying the girl,
I have enough to do in building myself up without
Looking after nineteen-year-old neurotic wretches.
And finally I reminded him, what is, in fact, the truth
That we are, in any case, both too old for the girl,
And he, moreover, wholly unsuitable.
This did not appear to comfort my poor friend,
Indeed he howled dismally and beat his head on the floor,
I could not see why.
So having done all that a reasonable man could to help him,
And having my advice rather brusquely rejected,
I went back to my Department and marked, for much of the
                                                    night,
Essays from students attending my course in Applied
                                                    Psychology.

7

Who rules the world, Professor?

Sadists, masochists, catamites, psychopaths, and Charley
                                        Demagogue.

Why is this so, Professor?

Because the people are sadists, masochists, catamites and
            psychopaths, and so vote for Charley Demagogue.

What can be done, Professor?

The people must he educated so that they will cease being
      sadists, masochists, catamites and psychopaths, and
      consequently will no longer vote for Charley Demagogue.

How can they be educated, Professor?

The sadists must be given a children's home to run riot in.
      This will re-integrate their impulses and teach them how
      to love their mother. The masochists must be whipped
      and thrashed at pleasure; severe cases may have one limb
      torn off and be beaten about the head with it; that should
      do some good. Oh yes, and catamites; here I am divided
      between inserting the tip of a gently warmed poker
      between the cheeks of the anus and giving a sharp
      upward thrust, or compelling them at pistol-point to go to
      bed with Jane Harbutt. Psychopaths are easy: the only
      hope for them is their instant destruction.

Then who will be left, Professor?

That is a stupid question. Even so I will answer it.
      Who will be left? Reasonable people,
      Reasonable people like me, you fool, like me, you
      fool, like me, you fool, like me...

161

12

It is very easy to learn how to be happy. All you do
Is go to the University of Auschwitz, knock at the door –
Room 101 – go in and ask for Grottmann.
You will then have more shit dealt out than you knew existed
As though the S.S. were crapping over your head
Having previously gorged themselves at a Roman feast.
You will get so low that they'll look for you under their bootsoles
When they want you they will simply pick up the hearthrug
Or peer beneath some flat stone
And find you curled in a foetal position.
But, rest assured, Grottmann is not mocked,
What Grottmann does will last you the rest of your life,
Which, after all, may not be long.
In time you will no longer know yourself,
And nobody else will care to.

Michael Horovitz

Resurrection of the Body*

spells
  buds   blossoms
    bugs   into butter
      flies
– death alone   dies   in the face
      of hot peace showers
flowering   unquestioned   space

  bird's in his heaven
  all's well with the worm
earth glows   continuous –
  a big snake curls up
the aisle – swishes & swings
to the electric   rock   of ages
the massed ark choir sings
& the animal   congregation   digs
its wondrous   sensate   infinity

  – pigs   dance with pigs
fish are jumping   heifers humping
  looney mice nibble
  at a vast moony cheese
  (traps   trap   traps)

  bride   groom   & babe
inter
  twine their blissful limbs
tasting the orb – man
                ball
      to womb
           head –
darting the root

hugging the trunk
  kissing the buds
    fearless shaking
    the tree of life
catching at – crunching
& sucking to the core
  the apples
  of knowledge
    as they fall
    to
      each other's
eyes

    – you can tell
  from those weird signs
  & subtle colours
  god's somewhere
    in on the scene
  but he's letting the devil
  sit in his throne
&   breathing deep   each
    & every
            one else
picks himself up
  – finds a fit place
blessed by
            her own
                  creation
– digs each
            their piece
of garden

where every
            body understands
seeded   in mutual   tenderness
 joined –
            many hands
make light work
                – make shine
the peaceable kingdom   flesh

*Note: this poem describes Michael Horovitz's (1996) painting of the same title.

Hard by Old Jewry

*"Yes: She fell four flights

...Her old man drew up just after
carrying a rabbit, the trefa thing
floppy ears hanging low, ragged
fur and legs – all freshly
gutted for the oven. He danced up
jaunty for cheers – hadn't been back
since years but *Hallo, I'm here –*
Light the gas and lay the table –
  Where are you dear? Dead
silence –   then to himself he muttered:
  What happens to wives? I should have
'phoned – I wonder... did she take
a lover? Or – what are those
– long black cars eeling
out of the narrow grey street
– What? A Shiva –
  Who? – My God, tell me – who
died? It seems tactless
shouting at us weeping women
and our men with torn lapels,
swart growths, the ash-stains everywhere
  – but he has to know, poor wretch:
    ...Dressmaker upstairs.
    – Oh no – no – ai... My love –
my wife...   And you mourn her? Were you
her friends? How long had she
been religious?
  I have wasted my life
he said. We never saw him again –"

**Note:* the speaker (recollected many years later) is a beturbaned Buba
akimbo in her Petticoat Lane doorway, circa 1960.

A Ghost of Summer

Where O where will wildness go
Now the sunshine turns to snow

The cold winds blow my spirits low
   The high winds call my spirit back

To flow and run – and ebb, for lack
Of clear direction.   Alone I walk

Through empty streets, I talk
To no-one – none else abroad

   My pumping heart awaits the hoard
Must needs reward me at the next hilltop

But mounted to the crest I stop
Aghast – no promised land in harvest there

Instead a maze of prostrate trees, picked bare
– Derelict dwellings   – Where went the crop?

   A labyrinth of ruined fields that tear
My hope out

         – Unidentified am I
A last seed blown nowhere by the wintry sky

for Modern Man (1914-1964) R I P

(Sparked by the graffito: 1914 – WAR
1939 – WAR
1964 – ?)

'Mentally he is on all fours... And what he fears most – God pity him – is his own image'
Henry Miller, *The Time of the Assassins*

'Humanity must perforce prey on itself like monsters of the deep'

King Lear

It's as if we were all
under the sea –
where the fallout of man
still implores
the downfall of manna –

'You don't know you're born' –
the things we used
to laugh at on the radio –

I remember hearing how in the Great War
(that's what they called it)
what was happening was quite clear
to nearly everybody.

In the Spanish war
George Orwell was about to fire
when he saw
his adversary had his pants down –

Seeing his cock – seeing him caught short – how ordinary
how could he but see
how absurd to kill –

168

You could at least sometimes see what you were doing
see your 'enemy' with your own eyes see
him seeing you –

But, I remember, such
mere human considerations
must needs
be over-
ruled:

Govern-
mental-political
hand-me-down blinkers – ideological
Vows-To-Thee-My-Country
were sufficient to outwit
evidence of the senses –

Patriotism dispenses
with 'the accident of'
human life

– And these days
look, the miracles of science
outwit
themselves:

An enterprising soft-drinks firm invents a carton through
which 'Hey

Fresko! You can *see*
what you're drinking now' –
And understanding of the atom has reached a pitch
where future generations of millions can be exterminated
alongside their descendants
at one fell buzz

– Shrieking *Capital! Commune*! Let *our* name reign
Gandhi die in vain – Bertrand Russell explain
to Socrates, Pope John
to God –

'Then kill, kill, kill, kill, kill, kill!'

'Howl, howl, howl, howl!'

– Would you rather die
badly, horribly
con-
    tin
    u
ous-
    ly
– or sever
the system. Say
No. Never.

Blast into oblivion the flags –
Disarm forever
the Eagle-Sickle-Swastika Crown.

   – My forefathers came from Hungary
where Horovitz was a town – a place, they said,
where most people lived outdoors
and died in bed – no hate, no dread –

But my parents – trouble enough, after nine kids already
  they had to bear
me – in Germany.
When I was two
the Nazis came –
we had to flee.

For that accident of birth it was... Fight the good fight
– You're a Jerry, they said at school, &
– You're a Jew, you go to Shul –

...'Hardpunch Horofist' I became & fought
for that same different me
– not for jolly Germany, not the Chosen race
for daily face to face I saw – each one of us
chosen for the human race
– its myriad individuality

Why fight   – if fight, fight for that – for you
and you and her and he
– fight for all humanity

Not in captivated fear – as moths flit about the light
– as though the atom were the monster
when it's we who have the power
to see – or cloud
the universe

a new flower – every day

...if we keep it on a human scale,
combat the darkness loud
– sink the doomboom might of bombers' flight

Unmourned mortality of a mushroom shroud.

Sonatina

How well and smartly bourgeois souls are tutored
to bow to the knell of Beethoven's dictates
and yet at times I'd scowl, '– I've *had* it
with old Ludwig: a child's reaction to the years
of being drummed between the ears that He's
the *Greatest* Greatest.
        Yet these days when
I happen on his loudly thumping highs
and rages, feeling his compulsions stretch and grip
the spine, to make us stop and march and stiffen –
chastened, primed – flex muscles and sing
    ...when hear repeats
    of those well-remembered clarion calls
that knock at conscience, lave all senses
to   – Resurgence! Liberty! Exaltations,
Apotheoses, over and over... the old glory
inflames me again;
        and then I remember how
– *Hammer-klaviered*, spirit-blasted into ecstasies
of race memory, prophecy, revolution – too
often we forget
        ......the gentle brook
of caresses opening – the Spring Sonata, the secret
spaces of our lives, now flooded with longing
at nightingale and cuckoo
recalled by clarinet trills, with

                flute-falls piercing

           far distances, that stillness
before a storm lets loose
  its dispassionate winds of change
  outside the concert's wall – as if
pre-ordained to wipe out the most precious
        ......quiet moments
    in whose fleeting air
the unwritten music of the heart can breathe.

Synagogue Music*

II

......In synagogue music
cantor and congregation,
cello and orchestra,
musicians and listeners
join
    in spirit-dance
spreading violin wings
weaving and humming, descanting,
spiralling – imageing limitless
    heights sublime...

Those who believe in it
get transformed
– uplifted as by lark-song
or the vision streaming through Bach chorales
or in Afro-American spirituals blazing
    their joyful noise unto the Creator.
Sometimes everyone present
seems to feel the call
to breathe deep, and fly
and sing like an angel
– yet earthed,
            pulse and heart
of race memory beating time
in a concerted living body of voices
bidding fair to out-reap death
– breath of past and future voicings held
together, swelling the refrains,
    chanting "Holy! Holy! Holy!"
      with such naked conviction, you'd think
        all hatred and evil would be dumbfounded
          – shamed to rot away
                  ...or turn round
        in redemption immemorial.

Sometimes you'd think the dreams
of a new world to come,
of Christ and Blake and all the others
dismissed as out-of-touch Utopians,
seem only natural
                                        – why can't
all the living
embrace *all* the living,
tend *all* the ailing,
mourn *all* our dead
in unison, keep faith
with our common prospect
of all souls
unborn, and reborn
freely giving, and forgiving
– old enmities revoked
in the will to live
without hate
  and share
  without fear
– replacing Babylon's wars, and Israel's
with a new, truly holy harmony?

...Not divided into 'chosen' and unchosen
when *every* mortal's chosen
for the human race – imagine it
declaring peace on itself,
healing for real
every Babel-cleft damned of nations
to walk together

                    "...and mutual build Jerusalem
                    both heart in heart, and hand in hand"

174

                          – naturally
extending family
                          – its children
                          and all their fruit
                          mothered, fathered
                          to grow freely, fully
in a whole different world
to come

as before
            the word
was begun,
            in the prospect
of a garden
by God,

so it tells us
the old song.

*This poem is from a seven-part sequence.

A.C. Jacobs

Poem For My Grandfather
On the Anniversary of his Death

Today, a candle in a glass
Burns slowly on the mantlepiece.
Wheesht, the dead are here.

My father, your grey-haired son,
Tastes again the salt, wax prayers
Of your sacred, dying day.

You are a name, holy in his presence,
The last solemn date
In our calendar of death.

Truly a ghost, my father sees, you.
A kind man's regret softens his face.

But for me there is no introduction:
For me you are a light on the mantlepiece,
A half shadow on the wall.

Report

Suddenly, I read in a newspaper
About an Arab poet,
Whose name I've never heard of,
Whose work I don't know,
In the land of Israel, in Palestine,
Fined, suppressed, threatened with imprisonment
For 'incitement',
And I want to shout:
Let his poetry survive in its valley
Making nothing happen,
Let him demonstrate his types of ambiguity,
Let him speak awkwardly, inadequately,
Like the rest of us,
For himself.

Mr Markson

That old man who came to teach me then
Has blended with many.
                  I can hardly remember now
Just what he looked like,
              except his black hat,
Yellowish stained beard, and shoulders hunched.
His accent too evades me
               except that it was broken
Like my grandmother's.

A dark, grey, distant, forgettable man,
Yet three times a week at the dining-room table
He would point to the curling Hebrew script
And pour into me all it said about Creation,
The fall of Adam, and the faith of Abraham.

There was a piety,
             and something more I couldn't
Understand in all that legend and recital:
A yearning in the old man's broken voice.

Travelling Abroad

Documents, scrutinies, barriers,
Everywhere I pass through them,
It seems, without difficulty.
Nothing jars, nothing slips out of place,
Authority is satisfied by my credentials.

Really, it must represent some peak
Of achievement, from a Jewish
Point of view, that is.
                  What a time
It's taken to bring me
To this sort of freedom,
What tolls have been paid
To let me come
                to this kind
Of passage.

I can appreciate it,
                believe me,
I can appreciate.

But I find myself wondering,
As I sit at this café table
                over
A good glass of beer,
Why I don't feel something more
                    like gratitude,
Why there's some form of acceptance
I don't grasp.

Visiting

It was fine visiting you in Cambridge.
I could see the soft misty elegance
Of that famous town in late November,
And who wouldn't recall a few at least
Of the great names harboured there.
                                                  We sat
In a bright hall opposite your college
                                        and listened
To an excitingly renowned American poet
Nervously probing his packed, tense lines.
                                        You deserve
All that the place can offer you,
                        all that mysterious learning
In store there.
                I was thinking that, as I walked
Back to the station, between the gentle buildings,
And passed a gang of youngsters, jeering
                        at a Japanese couple.

Booksellers

It hasn't taken long for even the street to go.
That crowded little street last time I saw it
Was smashed up and naked. Why should I mourn
Except for that bookseller who hoarded his volumes
There in a dark little shop, holy books and profane,
A transient collection brought over from the Continent
When such books were being torn and burnt, by decree?
Huge volumes of Talmud, small volumes of poetry,
Grammar and philosophy, guides for the perplexed,
The fruits of exile carefully reassembled
In another kind of ghetto.
                     After he died, I saw
His shop abandoned, ruined, opened to the illiterate air.
It had suffered a fire, and the burnt, soused collection
Lost touch with its identity.
                         Through the charred mess
I saw a fine copy of the stories of Mendele,
Writer of Yiddish, who called himself 'the Bookseller'.

Immigration

1

It wasn't easy getting out of the Tsar's Russia.
They had to bribe and lie.

And it was terrible on the ship.
They couldn't go up deck,
Someone stole all their luggage,
And the children were sick with fever.

Still, she came through it, my young grandmother,
And travelled to Manchester,
Where my grandfather was waiting, with a new language,
In Cheetham Hill.

2

Really, they'd wanted to reach America,
But never saved enough for the tickets,
Or perhaps it was just that their hearts were in the east,
And they could go no further west.

However it was, when Hitler went hunting,
We found that luckily
They had come far enough.

Region

On this side down through the trees
You come to the haugh, and the river
Flowing clearly over its stones.
                              The field
Across it leads up to the main road,
Duly numbered, signposted and flat.

And on the other side, if you go up
Alongside the burn, into the fields, you come
To a ridge where clumps of heather cling
And you can look down past the curving
Of the hills into the next valley.

                              Beyond those
More hills bulge up to the sky.
                              There are
Few buildings, byres mostly, or low cottages
In the distance.
                  On maps it is
All named, this place, accounted for.

But to me looking over it now
Towards the sunset
                        it is a nameless country
That could be mine.

184

Place

'Where do you come from?'
'Glasgow.'
'What part?'
'Vilna.'
'Where the heck's that?'
'A bit east of the Gorbals,
In around the heart.'

Alien Poem

I was born in a strange land.
Though I never invoked strangeness
The houses' grey walls
Of the town that was chosen
Kept back secrets, because of my lateness.

And though my father remembered
Other towns with trams and trees and silence
Their secrets, too
Would not be shared
With vagabonds, however respectable.

Strangers never grow into cities,
And their children encumbered with memories
Are clumsy, and afraid
They miss too much.
Sometimes, the strangeness is itself a promise.

In Early Spring

Walking in Hampstead in early Spring,
Where the patches of mud on the Heath
Reminded me of Winter's diseases no sun could get at,
I summoned my verses, such as they were,
To survey their afflictions and measure their promise.

And here in this cool English suburb
There grew in me the sound of all the singers
Who turned my people towards Jerusalem,
Or, hopeless in exile, mourned the loss of fulfilment
And the human errors that warped their love.

The Hebrew ones who clung to the purity
Of that vision that promised them return,
Yehudah Halevi, and Moses Ibn Ezra,
A man of love, whose learning served to make
A perfect poem, and know a bad one by instinct;

And afterwards Bialik who came near to seeing
What those ones in Spain knew only was a dream,
Though he knew too what centuries wound round their hearts
Enclosed his people in futility of words,
And rose and sang them out of stupor.

And also those whose sprawling anguish
Spread out in Yiddish across the grim frontiers,
And saw the tongue they nourished dying
Through what they too had longed for.
And those who in the many tongues of Europe

Were figures of exile, voices of victims,
Men torn by what they did not always know.
The ironic Heine, whose sharp sad lyrics,
Removed from the text-books, did not die
But ruined the Germans' perfect solution;

And tragic Rosenberg, whom a war killed
Before he got his great things into words;
My friend Jon Silkin; and those over the Atlantic
Looking at Europe like a distant curse.
And I hear most the miraculous, broken poems

That were made in the enclosures of insanity
Whose authors heard the chanting of the Inquisition
And smelt the smoke of the crematoria
And knew there was no escape, yet wrote
To show how life is at the verges of humanity.

Their great sound grew, and in that company
I walked past the pond and down the hill,
Aware that nothing was ended. With this Spring
They rose to a passionate renewal,
And I must serve their freedoms with my own.

'My Fathers Planned Me'

My fathers planned me with their prayers
And gave me their coded, ancient learning.
I heard their urgent voices where I walked,

But took my love in my arms
And found a human music in her voice
And named as joy what they explored with law.

We are a new people, she and I,
Whose lilts are pagan and have no appointed sound.
Away and far down my ghosts whisper a weak song.

N.W.2: Spring

The poets never lied when they praised
Spring in England.
                Even in this neat suburb
You can feel there's something to
                        their pastorals.
Something gentle, broadly nostalgic, is stirring
On the well-aired pavements.
                Indrawn brick
Sighs, and you notice the sudden sharpness
Of things growing.
                The sun lightens
The significance of what the houses
Are steeped in,
            brightens out
Their winter brooding.
                Early May
Touches also the cold diasporas
That England hardly mentions.

Untitled

Out among the dormitory towns
Of Buckinghamshire we took a wrong turning
And lost our way.
                        We stopped by a signpost
And discovered we were travelling
In a complete circle, without knowing how.
One of the girls made a joke about it
About us outside the ghetto, bewildered
In exile.
            Only a joke, of course.
                                    The fields
Of the Home Counties at twilight don't
Look that hostile, and we're well provided
With maps.
                It was just a small diversion,
And we soon hit the right road again

But that moment we stopped was awkward, maybe
More than we said.

Bernard Kops

Newlywed

When all the world was afternoons
that went on all the day,
our friends came round
to share our dreams,
and ate us out of house and home.
And so we moved away.

Diaspora

How sad that I have found nowhere,
that I have found no dream,
that I come from nowhere and go nowhere.

This is a land without dream;
an endless landscape.

Beautiful for those who can see their own sunset,
who can grow their own fruit out of their own sweat.
Beautiful for those in their own land,
whose laughter, whose tears soak into their own land.
Whose songs fill the earth and the sky of their own land.

How beautiful to dance and move and live and
dream and die in a country with a dream.

How sad I am that I have found nowhere.
My tears fall into the brick and haste and
death of day to day existence.

This is a country without dream
and no-one notices that I am crying.
By the waters of my own four falling walls
I wail.
I hear the trumpets, see the invisible
machines of destruction working in every corner.

How sad that I have found nowhere;
my son has no festival, this sun no ceremony.
How sad that the sea beyond does not lift me,
nor the hills.

Whatever Happened to Isaac Babel?

Whatever happened to Isaac Babel?
And if it comes to that –
whatever happened to those old men of Hackney
who sat around a wireless, weeping tears of pride
at weather forecasts from Radio Moscow?

Whatever happened to us? The Lovers of Peace?
And to our proud banners?
Whatever happened to our son?
And to that Picasso Dove of Peace
we brought back from Budapest?

Whatever happened to that little man
who tried to leap above himself?
He had a fire in his eyes;
a certain beauty in his eyes.
Or maybe that was merely poverty.

Whatever happened to Vladimir
Mayakovsky? Sergei Esenin? And Leon Trotsky?
Between the Instant Quaker and the Colour Supplement
we are apt to find no time to talk of them.

But then, we are apt to find no time to talk.

Now it is day,
and rather late in the day.
Whatever happened to us?

We are the worm contractors;
lusty youths of fire have become tweeded teachers,
with a swish Hi-fi that was bought for cash
and a smashing collection of Protest Songs.

O ye dreamers of peace!
Dreamers of a bright red dawn!
Whatever happened to that dream?

The dead are buried and the years
and forests of computers cover us.
We are crushed within the heart.
We are gone like prophet Leon
with ice-picks in our brain.

But there is no red stain.

We leave nothing behind
except volumes and volumes; such beautiful volumes.
Unread but rather splendidly
displayed upon tasteful teak.

O ye sitters down for peace!
Only the pigeons protest
these days down Whitehall.
O Comrades of Slogan Square!
This is a windy Judas corner;
this is the fraught, frozen over winter park.

I smile and walk backward.
If you insist I am also part of this.
But through my clenched teeth
I somehow cannot stop myself chanting.

Whatever happened to Isaac Babel?
Whatever became of me?

I think often of Isaac Babel,
of his unsung death.
And as I walk away from you
I know that I am all full up.
I am all full up with people.
I have no vacancies.

Suicide at forty would be mere exhibitionism.

Besides, I have songs to sing.
Songs for myself;
songs to keep me warm;
songs to feed into mouths.
And I have one mouth in particular to kiss;
and eyes above that mouth from where I draw my songs.
He was a funny little man, Isaac Babel.
And one would have thought him a nonentity,
had they not needed to dispose of him
so thoroughly in the dark.

Most people in this world are worthwhile;
therefore I can dispense with most of them.

You have to draw the line somewhere.

Yes, I think often of that little man
'with glasses on his nose and Autumn in his heart'.
Isaac Babel! Can you hear me?
I think often of your untelevised death.

Whatever happened to us
Returning from Whitehall
our banners smudged with rain,
our slogans running away?
Us waving, shaving, running after
our going youth and euphoria.
Hurtling through these fattening years
of hollow laughter.

And incidentally – who are we and
where are we?

So dreams die.
My dreams.
So can you blame me for building
barricades in West Hampstead?
Nice flat. Garden flat; un-numbered,
somewhere behind the Finchley Road.

With children laughing and children crying
and within me still one thread of longing.
And one wife calm and warm, belonging.

So – where was I?
Oh yes! Whatever happened to – ?
What was his name?

Never mind, nothing really changes;
except children grow,
and we realise there is nowhere else to go.
There is only us now. Us alone.

And not forgetting that rather funny
little Jewish Cossack fellow
whose name at the moment slips the mind.
Not to worry, they're bound to know
in Better Books.

There is a certain joy in knowing;
but then again a certain peace and quiet in
half forgetting.

For The Record

They came for him in Amsterdam; my grandfather David,
and with minimum force removed him from his house.

He surrendered to the entire German Army
and that was that.

It is of little consequence now;
so many die alone in foreign lands.
But for the record I must say
they gave him a number, helped him
aboard an east-bound train.

It was a little overcrowded,
but then again they had so many to dispatch.

You might call him part of the biggest catch
in history of those who fish for men.

Anyway, to cut a long story short,
he was never seen again.

I cannot put my finger on the exact day he died.
Nor the time, nor the place.

Suffice to say it was by gas and in the east.

I write this merely to record the facts
for my descending strangers.

Furthermore, today is the 21st of December
in the year of our Lord 1968.
And it is getting rather late.
It rained this evening but now the wind has dropped
and the moon is shining.
It is 11.33 p.m. Precisely.

Succot (Harvest Festival)

Today we will go to Regent's Park
with our daughters and our son.
We will stand beneath a chestnut tree
and aim as high as clouds
for conkers.

Our laughter will rise into the sky
above those clouds, higher
than those other sounds
our children do not seem to hear.

Then, hungry we shall hurry home
and spread our harvest all around the floor,
and I suppose we shall sing
for songs are the dreams
we capture from the dark.

Meanwhile all this will have to suffice
for miracles.

Diaspora II

I live in West Hampstead
where happy children
of all ages play
in all languages.
No windows are broken here,
no graffiti.
All in all a pleasant place.
But fears creep in;
fears that drip at three
in the morning.
They rap on the door of my dream,
and there in the night
the windows of my synagogue
are shattered.

Passover '38

One thing I remember
even more than the hunger.
Scrubbing my knees, smarting my hair and
rushing downstairs
into that playground of my childhood;
where all the other children
with their eyes alight
were building castles with crackernuts.

I built my castle.
I was a shopkeeper, a millionaire,
I ruled the world;
challenging all to chance
nuts of their own,
gathered from high pitched aunts
the day before,
as we went from home to home,
running that Yomtov gauntlet
of twisted cheeks and wet kisses.

In those days families extended forever and ever.

Who wants a castle?
Knock down my castle! I dared.
All in their sudden beauty
the girls came singing, flirting.
Holiday! Passover!
The Angel of Death? Who is he?
a madman on the radio, far away.

Passover lasted for the rest of the year;
the crackernuts secure
in the lining of my sleeve.
Belonging – we belonged.

Poverty came later,
when most of us did well
and moved away.

Our Friend Shirley

Our friend Shirley lives just behind Swiss Cottage.
Her face is like a mobile, travelling round
and around the room, never still.
Her eyes are poised somewhere in that no-man's land
between joy and sorrow.
Eyes that have seen it all
yet still are not tired.
Eyes that have witnessed Europe's tragedy
and her own.
Our friend Shirley is a good girl.
Often she brings us Bagels from Grodzinski
when she comes to call.
Our friend Shirley lives alone,
works hard, tends her little back garden,
and never phones us with her troubles.

Except this evening.

"...Guess what! You know that old girl,
the one who lives next door; the one I dress
every morning..."

Yes. She had told us.
Every morning, before she goes to work,
our friend Shirley, out of love,
goes down into that basement and helps
that old girl into a little dignity.

"...Guess what happened this morning?"

She died, I said.

"...No, much worse. That old girl made
anti-Semitic remarks as I was dressing her.
She cursed the Jews; said they were the cause
of this country's troubles. She said the Jews
were in control..."

What did you do? I said.

"...Never said a word. I dressed her and
I left. And I'm never going back. She can rot
in her bed as far as I'm concerned.
Do you blame me?"

No! And as I put the phone down I wondered
how that old girl would manage tomorrow
morning, without our friend Shirley.

Our Kids Have Just Left Home

We sit here rather dazed:
our kids have just left home.
We gave them all our love,
they raided all our dreams
and ate up all our jam,
and left us just like that;
laughed all down the road.
Our kids have just left home.
And oh the sweet relief,
come, let's postpone our grief
and please answer the phone.

They're coming three o'clock?
And staying far the night?
Where did we go right?

Max Ten Months Old

London. Winter. Time running out for this lost world.
How will we survive these virtual festivities?
Wet penetrating rain the only reality.
No-one will boldly come to seek us out and save us.
We are the voyeurs, running up the down staircase.
We celebrate this shortest day
searching, deifying Pagan godlings. Going plastic mad.
The fag end of the year.
Christmas. Goodwill to all men.
So what about women? No wonder they smile knives,
murder lurking in their knowing eyes.
Thank god we may not slide into the earth without screaming.
Christ mass! That's all we need.
How will we survive their saviour? How will we survive
these latter days? By stuffing ourselves for comrade worm?
Nietzsche said God is dead. I'm not feeling too well myself.
Friends explode. Relatives implode. The sky closes down.
Dark closes in.
Skeletons haggle over bankrupt stock in Oxford Street.
Halleluiah! Season of goodcheer for the undead.
Rabbis, priests lurk in doorway, practising popsongs.
Let's face it, we need a package deal to somewhere else.
Sweatless desperation.
Tubed. Work. Home to mortgage box. We come in
we pace for a while, then we go out.
All in all we needn't have been here.
You could say we've had it. It's too late.
But wait? See the one glimmer on the horizon.
There! In the afternoon my grandson Max!
Ten months old, claps his hands
kisses a moment of golden sun.
And all the darkness of doubt
and all the questions
and all the answers have no meaning.

And the universe and all the cosmic winds
of winter and the chill of endless night
ignite in a puff of laughter.
He lights up the sky.

Chloe

Out of the darkness of nothing
she arrived
pulling into this harbour
the shores of West Hampstead
as if not terrified
of the millions of aeons
that surrounded her journey
to us
She came by way of Diaspora Umbilica
taking in the songs and sorrows
of Odessa
the cries of Riga, Amsterdam
the sighs of Dublin
the winds of Dartmoor
And now she manages to sit up
with such delight
holding out her arms, staking her claim
to all of us with smiles.

Shalom Bomb

I want a bomb, my own private bomb, my shalom bomb.
I'll test it in the morning, when my son awakes,
hot and stretching, smelling beautiful from sleep. Boom!
   Boom!

Come my son dance naked in the room.
I'll test it on the landing and wake my neighbours,
the masons and the whores and the students who live
                             down-stairs.

Oh I must have a bomb and I'll throw open windows and
count down as I whizz around the living room,
on his bike, with him flying angels on my shoulder;
and my wife dancing in her dressing gown.
I want a happy family bomb, a do-it-yourself bomb,
I'll climb on the roof and ignite it there about noon.
My improved design will gong the world and we'll all eat
                                   lunch.

My pretty little bomb will play a daytime lullaby and
thank you bomb for now my son falls fast asleep.
My love come close, close the curtains, my lovely bomb,
   my darling.

My naughty bomb. Burst around us, burst between us,
   burst within us.

Light up the universe, then linger, linger
while the drone of the world recedes.

Shalom bomb

I want to explode the breasts of my wife,
and wake everyone,
to explode over playgrounds and parks, just as children
come from schools. I want a laughter bomb,

208

filled with sherbert fountains, licorice allsorts, chocolate
     kisses, candy floss,
tinsel and streamers, balloons and fireworks, lucky bags,
bubbles and masks and false noses.

I want my bomb to sprinkle the earth with roses.
I want a one-man-band-bomb. My own bomb.

My live long and die happy bomb. My die peacefully of
     old age bomb,
in my own bed bomb.
My Om Mane Padme Aum Bomb, My Tiddly Om Pom Bomb.
My goodnight bomb, my sleeptight bomb,
my see you in the morning bomb.
I want my bomb, my own private bomb, my Shalom bomb.

Lotte Kramer

The Tablecloth

A tablecloth,
A white, coarse linen weave,
A dead thing, so it seems.
Its threads are gently rent
In places, as in dreams,
When falling into pits
We wake in unbelief.

So frays this weft.
My father's mother made
The cloth in quiet days.
What patient thoughts she wove
Around this loom, narrow
Village ways, important
Hours underlined her shade.

Now, when I touch
This fragile web, and spread
It with our wine and bread,
And watch it slowly die,
I grieve not for its breach
But for the broken peace,
The rootlessness, our dread.

April Wind

Here, under the sky's wide wheel
The wind sharpens the day's blade.

April has come with abrupt
Harshness, mocking the shy sun,

Blazing the blossom's softness
Over the shivering grasses.

Shadows are as restless as
Nervous fingers, unable

To find the day's knot and measure;
Bullfinches, in a sudden fit,

Sit and strip our apple-tree
Of buds – so much destruction

Unrolling in this low land;
An augury of rough spring

Falling on hill country, one April,
Years ago, when the breaking

Of glass stunned my grandfather's
Heart, not dead, in this wind's cry.

Equation

As a child I began
To fear the word 'Jew'.
Ears were too sensitive.
That heritage was
Almost a burden.

Then broke the years of war
In a strange country.
This time they sneered at me
'German' as blemish,
And sealed a balance.

Grandmother

She could walk no further
 Than the garden gate,
Her black skirt dusting hot sand;
 Where the yellow heat
Bent down to us as it spanned
 – From a sunflower's face –
Her slowing bones that belied
 Her agile eyes.

In their brightness quickened
 Eighty years of life:
The wisdom of long widowhood;
 The time of briskness;
The stride to the waterpump;
 To the bales of cloth
She had wound and unwound like
 Multi-coloured snails.

Her look hunted hardship:
 That barbed-wire gaze
That had governed her five sons
 Still ruled without words
From a filigree frame.
 And the linen she wove
With a sun-shy hand still cools
 And calms my face.

Diaspora

Rivers – we are –
Glass mothers,
Bearing the slow barge
With its cargo of coal
From the sea's cleft throat,
To the mountain's broad heel.
There, where the water
Knuckles its knee,
By rivalry
Of bridges,
We stayed a while,
A thousand years.

Not for us:
The constancy
Of roots, of black trees
Charcoaled in deep clay;
Nor the ochre-brown stone
Carved into the slate cloud.
But we, too, return,
Altered in movement,
In the same God's
Drenching air,
And the same light
Haunts our hands.

At Dover Harbour

Behind this rough sleeve of water
There lies the heart's island, set in
A harvest of stone, its work done.

Ahead, the broad hand of Europe
Opens her lined landscape, the skin
Hard and calloused with bitter blood.

And the arm heaves under grey cloth
Releasing the split signal of
The lighthouse of love with its white

Exploding star, turning always
In the black wind that calls me back
To whispering benedictions.

The Hour

The wire mesh of trees across the street
Tells of a garden now in winter dark,

An empty kitchen's whiteness underneath
Hangs in a basement as suspended life.

No sound creeps through this Sunday afternoon
When windows can be satisfied with light

In a suburban house. Air sleeps alone.
And somewhere now there are the frozen ones,

The old, the lovers without gestures, bled
And bored with such a day. – As quietness

Loops round and round the room, brushing at fear,
It almost prays, almost implores the desk,

The lamp, the chair, to brandish words inside
Another hour's question and retreat.

New Year's Eve

We hardly noticed that old knotty tramp
Wolfing his food (a place near Leicester Square)

Until there crossed a steel of voices, rush
Of shoes: 'Two pounds you owe us, you'll not go

Before you've paid!' He rumbled broken words,
Half sentences, tried running to the door

But fists came clamping down to trap him, push
Him to the basement stairs; one final kick,

Threat of police, was all we heard. Cowards,
We were, who sipped the year's last cup of tea

In silent fellow-travellership when faced
With hunger, cruelty, our undone deeds.

Power Cut

Suddenly the television died
That late Sunday afternoon
When dusk threatened into dark:

Unused to shadowless silence
I hunt for candles
Stowed away for years

In some understair hold;
Distant 'safe rooms'
Plugged against poison.

I bleed white wax into saucers
On the kitchen table,
Huddle by the gas oven's lit throat

And read flickering words
Of poems that leap up
In triumph over this muteness.

From our cavern I watch
How blackness intensifies
Punctured by flashlights of cars

As we slide deeper into night
With its blur and footsteps,
Take comfort in uncertainty

Of the almost limbo
Where loss congregates
On the far side of sleep

Until, in an explosion of light
Noises intrude and demand
The deep-freeze whines again.

Cocoon

She says she can't remember anything
Of people, language, town; not even school
Where we were classmates. Her smile is frail
And hides behind her husband's hypnotising

Quietness. 'A Suffolk man' he beams,
And squares his tweedy frame against some
Unseen advocates who might still claim
An inch of her. She is content, it seems,

To lose her early childhood; he is near.
Protector or destroyer, it's his war.
He underwrites her willed amnesia,
Helps her to stifle terror, exile, fear.

She is cocooned, safe as an English wife,
Never to split that shell and crawl through love.

Oxford, 1940s

Then I was "Mother's Help – Lady's Companion",
A teen-age girl in love with fantasies
Walking the wartime Oxford streets and lanes.

The colleges were locked facades to me
Quite out of bounds with military use
But still regarded with romantic awe

As territories one day to be explored
By one who'd shed the enemy alien skin.
Meanwhile there were the books – some treasured

Second-hand, picked up at Blackwell's for a song.
An early Schnitzler with the spine in shreds
And hinted sex in dashes worming through

To savour secretly. Before permissiveness.
Long, lonely afternoons up Shotover,
The hill that took me past an empty church

I sometimes entered, praying in my search
For something new and weatherproof
But never found. Years looking for a clue.

A cleric gave a lecture, gaunt, severe,
On faith, a Puritan of sorts, a Scot
Who sent me down a draughty corridor

A mile or two. Not very far. 'Macbeth'
Came to the theatre and filled my head,
My bones and bloodstream ever since, the breath

Of witches stoking up my words. A flame
As permanent as air. And British
Restaurants would earn their wholesome name

With calories that lined my ribs. U.S.
Canteens were treasure troves that sometimes
Spilled their gems. And war was somewhere else.

Disused Railway Line

Rusting and bereaved
Of the weight of wheels
The celibate line
Ladders the horizon.

Crows black-button
The grass at intervals
Depressing frost
That has sugared its blades.

We follow this flat
Staircase, aware
Of dead journeys
To destinations

Crumbling with unuse.
We negotiate gaps
In a museum of steam
Painting the sky white

As wildflowers recover
Hesitant faces
In sooty soil
Remembering their roots.

Joanne Limburg

A Lesson in Ballooning

First of all – the instructor said –
we should forget the myth we'd learned
in school that only the best could fly.

Quite the opposite was true
and by the end of the morning everyone
in that room would rediscover

her God-given power to leave the ground.
He smiled at us, a nodding circle
of earnest girls in ethnic skirts,

split us into groups of four
and took the lid off his marker pen.
I admit I was sceptical at first:

the uplifting quotes I could take or leave,
the hugging just embarrassed me
but then, quite abruptly – just before coffee –

I felt the ground release my feet...
...and I was up with a rush of air:
easy as stepping out of a shoe

to shed the room, the building, the street
and rise until the London I'd left
was just a teeming *A-Z*.

The city's asthmatic wheeze grew faint
as I breathed in the pure, blue
laughing gas of almost-heaven.

Dusk fell. I drifted lazily
over the green belt. Then I discovered
that I couldn't feel my toes;

had slipped, quite gently, out of my skin
like a tomato in boiling water.
At once I was vomiting sunset

as if I were a spoilt birthday
girl, puking up the trifle.
The whole of the sky was my head and it ached.

Suddenly I was nostalgic for ceilings,
yearning for home, with all its walls
and for someone to break my upward fall.

The Nose on My Face

Someone hopes I don't mind
them asking, but am I –?
                              Suddenly
I'm sixteen again, spending
hours in front of my parents' mirror,

holding my hand across the middle
third of my face, admiring
the inoffensive adequacy
of my eyes and mouth, when

they weren't being overshadowed
by my nose, that was so...
What was it about my nose? Did it
have a pushy way of forcing

itself into a room, a vulgar
nose-come-lately, embarrassing
and overdressed? Did it mark
its owner as a fleshy, suburban

princess condemned to a life of shopping
and eating and smothering sons? Was it
transparently over-emotional? Was it
lubricious, dishonest or dirty? Would it

forever spite my face, the kind
of nose that would tell the world that –
                              Yes,
I say. I am. And someone says
that's funny, they'd never have guessed.

Mother Chicken Soup

God forbid
her family should starve,
so mother is boiling herself down
for soup,

slicing the carrots
with an upward stroke to the thumb,
rolling perfect *kneidlach*,
mixing up the stock.
After so many years
nothing needs to be measured.

Hasn't she been rehearsing this
for years?
Divided herself, leg and breast,
one, two, three ways
to make three children's mothers?
Put aside her book,
her job, her time?
Taken the food off her own plate
a thousand times?

The oven clock pings.
Time to dissolve her life into theirs,
dive into the broth.

She listens for the other mothers
calling from the pot
then jumps in,
neatly, as she does everything.

Neatly, she has left a note
by the fruitbowl:
'I don't expect gratitude –
only that you should do as much
for your own children.
Turn me up to 150
when you get in. Mum.'

Seder Night with any Ancestors

On this night,
my ancestors arrive,
uninvited but expected,
to have their usual word.

They sit around the table
but refuse my offer of food.

I switch the television off
and wait,
the air thickening
with disapproval.

At last I ask them:
What do you want from me?
What have you got to do with me?
Why do you come here, every year
on this night?

And what do they say?

They say:
For this God brought us forth from Egypt?
For this we starved in the desert?
For this we fled the inquisition?
For this we fled the pogroms?

Did we die
refusing unclean meat
for you to fill your fridge with filth?

Did we disguise
our Hebrew prayers
with Christian melodies
so that you could forget them?

For you we did these things?
Do you think the Lord
would have thought you worth saving?

I say that all I want
is to live my life.

Without us you would have no life.

Maternity

I saw out my father's funeral
a shocked guest in my own home,
drinking and passing
one endless cup of tea,

PG Tips! He'd never let that in the house.

and sat on a low chair
doing nothing for myself,
helpless as a queen bee,

He should've taken better care of himself.

while the living-room buzzed
with kissing cousins and rabbis
and old long-sighted neighbours,

He was so dashing – I remember his red MG.

taking calls and opening doors and feeding me.
First they brought an egg,
then a bagel, for the roundness of life,

Only last week he was telling me a joke.

and then they filed past
planting the seeds
to germinate a father.

He had such knowledge, but he wore it so lightly.

Since then I've eaten for two,
feeling that other person come together
face and voice, inside me.

232

He was beautiful.

Soon I'll know him, keep him
as thoroughly as any unrequited love,
or longed-for stillborn baby.

Emanuel Litvinoff

To T.S. Eliot

Eminence becomes you. Now when the rock is struck
your young sardonic voice which broke on beauty
floats amid incense and speaks oracles
as though a god
utters from Russell Square and condescends,
high in the solemn cathedral of the air,
his holy octaves to a million radios.

I am not one accepted in your parish.
Bleistein is my relative and I share
the protozoic slime of Shylock, a page
in Stürmer, and, underneath the cities,
a billet somewhat lower than the rats.
Blood in the sewers. Pieces of our flesh
float with the ordure on the Vistula.
You had a sermon but it was not this.

It would seem, then, yours is a voice
remote, singing another river
and the gilded wreck of princes only
for Time's ruin. It is hard to kneel
when knees are stiff.

But London Semite Russian Pale, you will say
Heaven is not in our voices.
The accent, I confess, is merely human,
speaking of passion with a small letter
and, crying widow, mourning not the Church
but a woman staring the sexless sea
for no ship's return,
and no fruit singing in the orchards.

Yet walking with Cohen when the sun exploded
and darkness choked our nostrils,
and the smoke drifting over Treblinka
reeked of the smouldering ashes of children,
I thought what an angry poem
you would have made of it, given the pity.

But your eye is a telescope
scanning the circuit of stars
for Good-Good and Evil Absolute,
and, at luncheon, turns fastidiously from fleshy
noses to contemplation of the knife
twisting among the entrails of spaghetti.

So shall I say it is not eminence chills
but the snigger from behind the covers of history,
the sly words and the cold heart
and footprints made with blood upon a continent?
Let your words
tread lightly on this earth of Europe
lest my people's bones protest.

To a Best Selling Novelist

You who cherish the word and prize the white lily
yet relish the easy corruption of roses,
surrounded by cherubs and the children
still dumb in your heart, who in the electric glare
of big banquets must pretend
the shy-faced moon a jolly gentleman,
are urbane and always an 18th century wit.

But I see a young shepherd, David,
the singer, who descended the dreamy mountain
and slew no giant, but spoke tenderly
of the bazaars:
how he was enchanted by the miraculous city
his harp had conquered, and how
wooed with cunning a handful of praise,
the patted head. Though the blank years filled with books
and his name grew legends in all the tongues of Babel,
he was never older than sixteen, never more than a boy
whose mouth was sticky with the illicit sweets
squeezed from the shy sex of flowers.

May no chill weather make his singing dumb
nor darkness quench his eighteen carat sun,
but let that princely ornament remain.

For a New Generation

We set out together a day's journey from home,
but our footprints left no mark on the waters
and a million stars bewildered our compasses.
Yet old men still called Jerusalem with reedy sorrow
a long way over strange mountains and died
pointing their feet toward Sinai.
Sick with knowledge, being not wholly sane
nor having the purity of madness, it seemed
we were marooned in the last country,
exiled from the scriptural valleys, the hills
scrolls unread; and in all our fugitive babylons
no song like Solomon's, no marvellous voices
ringing among the disputatious prophets –
go here, go there, and the hard roads leading nowhere:
a journey as farcical as Jonah's.

So in the time of living in borrowed cities
our harp turned melancholy as soft rain,
adept at a sad song in the blue dens of night.
Moses, of distinguished lineage, an impresario
of tragedy, cast as patriarch;
Solomon, a collector of antiques but somewhat sinister,
neatly turns a compliment to ladies
as befits so sybaritic a temperament; and in the East
strange Jews burn like tapers with an unfashionable piety.
And all go down into the belly of History.

Then suddenly the Lord stops laughing:
the joke and the journey had gone, perhaps, too far.
Return, return, though all the seas are red,
discard the foreign face the strange singing voice,
and I shall make a Jerusalem more lovely than any.

Many indeed seek to recover their lost innocence
beneath the cracked mosaic and Byzantine ruins;
some wear the shepherd's cloak with almost natural grace;
but many cannot lose the habit of exile
though the hills of Judea run down to the same sea
and the old vocabulary is printed on the sky.
Having been transient on many soils,
have they not learned the singular virtue
of the sun that nourishes thistle and barley
and orders the mineral destiny of planets
though minute cities are puffed away by the wind?

Israel is a marriage between youth and the soil
and we, who cannot easily unlearn our loves,
dream that this land may unburden you of history;
and in that absolution from the past
the gangrened breast of earth will heal
and the desert yield its buried harvest.

The Hunted Stag

For who shall speak for the dead who have no tongue?
And who shall speak for the quick who have no wisdom?

Running with dread of winter in the bone
or with the urge of spring, the panting stag,
devoted to his trees, quiet in his forest,
tosses his antlered scorn into the air,
his muscular swift form betrayed
to the still inconsequence of death.

Then comes the unquiet wind empty of grieving
fretting the branches of his waiting woods
who know him better for the solitude that broods
upon his absence than for his call
subtle in season for his summer's need:
then comes the wind and all is forgotten.

Only the hunter perpetuates with pride
the unstaunched blood of innocence betrayed,
surveys his triumph and his dead accuser
unmoved by silence of the tender mouth,
not knowing that a fine spring like a hair
is broken from its place among the stars,

Nor that the steadfast sun will melt like wax
when blood has summoned blood in raging heat
and every river dries up at its source.
Where are the strong who can defy the weak?
The conquering stranger is most vulnerable
who cannot conquer what is undefended.

And none can wrest his speechless agony
as prize: the hunger burning in his hollow gut
craves blood and poison, for his loveless past
marries no gentle future. Let him take
what can be taken; all will be forgotten but
the wind's unquiet in the brooding woods.

The Orator

Wherever herds were gathered he was there,
part actor and part priest, to loose his words
like sheepdogs growling at their heels
in service to his master, the Occasion:
apt as an epigram, his eloquence
alone could complete an act of history and,

Born with a gluttonous appetite for speech,
his tongue could drip a poisoned honey
sweet to the ear but fatal to the heart,
fling epithets like bullets against peace,
gild greed a golden virtue, lust a lily
blooming for heroes among the Sabine

Women. His rich voice sweetened on corpses:
deep and thrilling, he could meet their praise
with lush and laurelled dignities, raise
verbal cenotaphs to close their violence.
The brave thunder of his guns in war
shamed the inglorious reproach of grief.

What did it matter if his metaphors
were frayed and mildewed like a sack of rags?
He knew the magic of old spells could bind
a power of hate upon his ancient curses,
and he could patch and mend his purple cloak
to prove the repetition of events.

Walking in space he dread to touch the ground
and lose his pain in commonplace commotion,
rather would he be a bronze bell ringing
carillons for victory and harvest or,
better still, toll the bruised silence
falling like ash on the spent field of war.

241

Poem for an Heretical Avenger

Deep down the dumb wound speaks,
the brass-tongued bells
rebound against stone hills,
hammer the ears of valleys and
blow up the voice of thunder
to the holy rock-towering peaks
of the law-giving mountain.

Moses, son of the river, of the bitter
blood-drinking Nile,
irascible tender father bound
by the great tyranny of sight
and the burden of words
to the end
to the end of the world,

O in the loneliness of your heart
where the fall is revealed
and the redemption pierces
the bloodstained shroud of history,
the Word is growing to release us,
the Word grows huge and starshaped,
a five-pointed man whose centre
glows hot as the hurt of a sun.

That anguish multiplies the praise,
the glowing charcoal of the fire-
scorched flesh subsides to ash
but the flaming tongue leaps on
from twig to branch to burn
among the trees its livid blossom
and to roar with sacred vengeance
through the streets of incandescent
cities: the earth ignites
and all the buried centuries compressed
like coal beneath the crust of time
blaze up and burn an augury in the sky.

Earth and Eden

Where time and memory intersect the sun
seeds of the wise tree grow about our roots;
where space and conquest spread upon the earth
our wisdom is undone.
Within us thoughts like wild years unwind,
emotion moves upon us like a storm,
desire waxes like forest fire, and quietly
consuming dark spreads stealthily the sky.

These intersections are remoter patterns,
than pain familiar to the pleading flesh.
World of abstractions grown immaculate
recedes far from the hand of hate,
the loins of love.

Lying together, man and woman lie
far as the separated islands of the sea,
shoulder to shoulder as the comrades stand
there is an abyss of divided lands.
We are disorder, all our fretful nerves
cry of division like the separate stars,
friend and our enemy, stranger and brother,
heart of our loving knows no unity with mind.
Where is the synthesis?

There is a tragedy of simple hearts
who go believing to appointed death;
there is disaster of the wise,
belief and unbelief war in their minds –
but no firm order of the rising sun,
phases, inevitable, like the growing moon,
four natural seasons of the patient earth;
one is a multitude given to strife.

In root there lies the pattern of the flower,
we seek our purpose who have sprung from seed
and make death like a carnival
of lost and wayward purposes.
Progressively confusion we achieve
who would impose the power of our will.
These are the agonies we lay upon ourselves –
the final pain, the dazed and unconsidered sorrow,
death, love's negation.
And so, bewildered, do we beg our prayers.

Where time and memory intersect the sun
there is our happiness, there
in the still and burning centre
is the synthesis.

If I Forget Thee

Alone in this desert under the cold moon
spilling its thin blood of a ghost
dimly among the voices of my grief
how can I give you my life's love
alone in this desert I cannot map
where perhaps we wandered with our common father
towards Jerusalem our proud punishment?

Do not think I can forget
or my laugh be careless ever
that I shall look upon old hands
or young faces without remembering
O do not think the white face of Moses
staring down from a mountain
invokes no resolution.

Others may bind you in the still
map of silence
blind your great eyes with discs
others may forget
perhaps Ptolemy following his planets round
saw how you fell burning
among the incandescent demon stars
and forgot his horror
but O my children how can I forget?

One day my love will find
a road over the desert and my joy
will blossom among you like primroses
one day you will see me with my hands
filled with flowers sprung from the desert
your death made fertile and
I shall crown your innocent heads
with twelve stars of Israel.

Israel

We have broken bread in many places,
under dark cellars in cities shunned and
   gloomy corners,
where the damp continent meets the gutter,
where Babylon is buried and the learned tablets
meet with sand; and, as rivers slowly dried,
the golden valleys turning hollow as quiet ghosts,
where the lights went out
we have broken bread.

In Europe now, under the black cross,
the holes in Vienna gather shadows leaning
out of a pyramid, draw together rags and purple
appointing glory to the wan child,
the Polish village, draughty as a skeleton,
turns to Jerusalem from the hushed terrible wind,
the old and changeless voice of the wilderness,
the Lord, the Lord is One.

Whatever happens to us, happens,
we cannot speak our words, only the Word.
We are not ourselves; disposing of everything,
flesh, mind, the body's rapture of desire,
something remains of us, but not ours.
Often, believe us, it would be sweet to die,
not to feel this intolerable pain of history
to suffer no more for the Name
written in our eyes, stemming from blood and flesh
our mother and father formed in ritual.
Often we would become children of no identity,
no history: but the knife is withdrawn from the
   pierced heart,
time flows under the ribs and spills
no drop of knowledge.

Who among us has not searched his eyes
and heart of childhood
finding under the young grass soil and psalm
of centuries? Who has not heard the first gibe
echo and grow clamorous with martyrdom?
Who has not endured the shuttered door and
 binding laws
In many times of wandering?
And who, hearing gibbet and cross of torment,
has not borne the stigmata in his flesh?
In being branded Christ and pharisee,
who can deny his Moses and the Father's prophecy
knowing the meeting of the two,
glory and shame in one fierce crucible?

We have learnt to submit, to break
a crust under the lean time.
We discover rejoicing as the wheel crushes
our bones, flowering ecstasy in pain.
Once act of will, now sufferance releases prophecy.
Having seen God consume the bush,
knowing fire consumes us too and never
destroys immortal tissue, we bend
beneath the black frost of Europe, losing branch and leaf
and through the bare and mutilated tree
the wind, the changeless voice of wind, whispers
the Lord, the Lord is One.

End of an Episode

For those who sit stooped as a dying race,
a circle in the mud traced by their finger
round symbol of their end and history,
to be futureless is a last act of grace
as death is the merciful end of hunger.
There is a season when the years hang ripe
and purple, when it is easy to make love
under the vine of time; there is a harsh season
when the mouth is too hard for kisses, the frost too deep:
there is a year when the clocks are stopped
at the last disaster.
Then what is left is so much dust, ash
from a crucible, the dry residue of a heart
that measured time one instant of grief too long –
and only the final blow whose fall
is a bitter benediction.

Gerda Mayer

The Agnostic's Prayer

God, to whom I'm still inclined to
say my prayers, though God knows why,
guard me, if you have a mind to,
while I here abandoned lie.

I depend on your good nature.
Irony leads me astray.
Save the world, God, save your creatures,
save us for a rainy day.

Thank you for your grace and favour,
though the memory's remote.
Keep my cat safe, keep my neighbour's,
keep them from each other's throat.

Toad

Toads, toads, your place is full of them
you complain, & what do I see
but a small toad slip from your mouth &

H^{O}P H^{O}P

over your beer & onto the floor
I ignore it the way one does

But how do I ignore
the vast stonecoloured toad in the centre of my house
where you deposited it where you spat it out
it sits   it sits
ancient and unshiftable
two thousand   murderous   years in weight

God Wot

"A garden is a lovesome thing, God Wot!"
T.E. Brown

Left over from the Flower-arranging class,
Stuck in a jar donated by Pottery,
They pose before us, wilting, a sorry bunch.
We dip the brush for some God-Wottery.

Mabel and Barbara dutifully attempt
To paint them for the lovesome things they were,
To me they're in a carriage pointing East,
And wave thin hands, and fight for the fetid air.

The tulip's ripped, the wallflower underfoot,
But I lack the talent and nerve to portray them thus:
Though I know their names; though I know their faces
                        and names.

Forgetmenot, you're rendered anonymous.

Carve Me Up When I Die

Carve me up when I die
I bestow myself
on these various places:

My skull to my dentist
so that my full
set of teeth
may beam its
thanks on him.

My heart shall be placed
under the brick
by the rose,
to join Pip my cat.

Put my hands in a muff
somewhere under the
lazy daisies.
They shall be
bone idle.

Bury my tongue and my ears
well away from each other:
so that my ears
need not be afflicted
by the tale of my life
told over by the tongue.

And put clay into my ears.
They above all wish to die.
Let no sorrowing sound
reach them.

As for the rest of me,
let the sea have it.
Let it enjoy the sea.

Except for my feet.
Send them back into childhood.
Bury them in the garden there.

Make Believe

Say I were not sixty,
say you weren't near-hundred,
say you were alive.
Say my verse was read
in some distant country,
and say you were idly turning the pages:

The blood washed from your shirt,
the tears from your eyes,
the earth from your bones;
neither missing since 1940,
nor dead as reported later
by a friend of a friend of a friend...

Quite dapper you stand in that bookshop
and chance upon my clues.

That is why at sixty
when some publisher asks me
for biographical details,
I still carefully give
the year of my birth
the name of my hometown:

GERDA MAYER born '27, in Karlsbad,
Czechoslovakia... write to me, father.

The author's father, Arnold Stein, escaped from the German concentra-
tion camp in Nisko in 1939, fled to Russian-occupied Lemberg/Lwow and
then disappeared in the summer of 1940. It is thought he may have died
in a Russian camp.

Children With Candles

The children are the candles white,
Their voices are the flickering light.

The children are the candles pale,
Their sweet song wavers in the gale.

Storm, abate! Wind, turn about!
Or you will blow their voices out.

The Emigration Game – Winter 1938/39

Mother and I walk through the streets of Prague.
Her hands are balled against the falling snow.
(Can't she afford gloves? Are they bare from choice?)
There's snow above and endless steps below.

We have a bag of chocolate-creams; we play
The Emigration Game: England, if brown;
Or, if the centre's white, we must stay here;
If yellow, it's Australia. Snow falls down.

I pick a brown and mother has the white.
She walks with a straight back: let's try again.
Her legs are varicosed; her heels are raised.
She's bearing up and stout of heart. In vain

From consulate to consulate her steps
Inscribe petitions. Soon the sweets are gone.
Then March comes and invaders bar all routes:
Yet leave no trace of her when they move on;

Their footsteps beating time and bearing down.

Jeremy Robson

The Promised Land

"It can't be done"
they told us
shaking knowing heads
"don't try to fight"

They were right
it can't be done
we tried

And now we have become
pilgrim clouds
searching for the heavens
of a promised land

The Departure*

We spoke tonight
of the departure from Egypt
Climbing down the spiral of the years
Trailing our minds over the desert
Over the Sea of Death over the Promised Land
Over the might of Moses toppled
in the harvest of his field.
We sang tonight
chanting the ancient ageless songs
the wailing of a People
crumbling the barrier of the years.

Over the cities of the world hung our songs
Over the abyss of the centuries hung our words.

We opened our doors
for Elijah, Elijah the Prophet
but prophetically he was forewarned and frightened;
they are all frightened
Prophets
Prophets are crucified
only Hitlers are heard
shrieking damnation.

And soon our songs hung silent
over the cities of the world.
Soon the tongues stood still
And the dust settled again
On the pavements of prayer.

*On Passover evening, services are held by the Jewish people in their
homes to recall the exodus from Egypt.

Waking
for Carole

Waking, you said you saw your house,
the Nile snaking into mist,
Mohammed the one-eyed cook.
Somehow, you said, there were children,
running...

And I have watched you waking,
breaking from an Orient
half-hinted at in gestures, frowns
a craze for things with spice,
pepper, pomegranate, pimento, rice,
love of the desert, rock, the open sky.

And in you, grave refugee,
I catch an ancient plight:
not crammed in trucks
not stoned on sight
hounded by Inquisition
or crusading zeal,
but turned
without word without sound
from shore to sea: Suez '56 –
a Cairo-born French-speaking
Spanish Jewess on the wing.

It was wonderful, marvellous, you say
the late sun thumbing the Nile
the children running...
And away you go into dream:

the new London day dismissed
the four safe walls,
the friend that guards, regards you,
comes so close, retreats,
hearing a voice troubled in sleep
calling a new name, in a strange tongue,
distant and complete.

Pete Seeger at the Roundhouse

You brought us songs from the Spanish soul,
pure, loud voices of the peasant's labour.
Guantanamera: I am a truthful man.

From Little Rock, Montgomery, Birmingham,
charged songs of the Freedom Fighters.
We shall not, We shall not be moved.

From black German camps, Dachau, Belsen,
you brought hope, the human voice rising in song.
Up and down the guards are pacing.

In Turkish, Yiddish, Bantu, French,
gentle man, you brought us strength,
and on that stark, freezing night, a roof.

Meeting

There were the words you did not say
Fräulein, your wild hair back
in the Dietrich way, arms
outstretched on a rising, falling cross –
one two, one two: faceless
troops from the faceless trains
ghosts of the dead camps still untamed.

Doubtless it was the silver cross
you wore tore us away, two lovers
silent on the sheets that day.
I, Caesar's legions dead in Judean dust
recalled, starred *Shadai* on my rising chest:
you, the final cry of a Christ betrayed.
My God, my God...
Two silver chains gave us away.

Between You and Me
for my grandfather

Like sentinels we wheeled
you along paths, across fields
to a space beside a fence.
Everything you loathed was there:
grave clothes, grave countenances

dull women in even duller hats
the pomp and high-pitched
words you'd have topped
with a not-so-quiet aside.
Yet we were with you

all the way, your silent Tribe
and when the clods dropped,
shattering the day, a bird flew
and something final snapped.
Moving on, beyond the strangers'

stares, Shakespeare on my tongue
Beethoven in my head, I knew
I'd find you there, not here
amidst this black business.
One image sticks: a coffin

draped in a chandeliered hall,
mirrors uncovered, the usual
lights ablaze: to the left, poised
a puzzled, watching bronze
and beside you, smiling down

your Sickert "Dancing Girls"
their right legs raised.
As the service droned, yes
I know you caught their eyes,
smiled back true to form, winked.

264

Michael Rosen

The Wedding

Uncle Ronnie got married in *shul*
my dad was the best man
there they all were standing under the *khuppe*
and the Rabbi is talking
and *Bubbe* is watching from her wheelchair
and it's time for my dad to hand Ronnie the ring.

Out it comes and just as my dad gives it to him
Ronnie faints.
Out cold.
Bubbe starts crying,
and everyone in the *shul* starts talking and tutting.
So Eileen's brother got his shoulder in tight on Ronnie
on one side
and my dad got his shoulder in tight on Ronnie
on the other
and the *shammes* propped him up from behind
and that was Ronnie's wedding.

Bubbe said later it was a terrible shame
he missed it.

Trying to be Jewish 1

When I was seven
David Kellner came up to me at school and said,
You are aren't you?
What?
No, you are, I know you are, you are aren't you?
I'm sorry, I don't know what you mean, I said.
My mum says you are and she knows,
she says she knows you are from your name.
What?
You're Jewish aren't you?
I think so, I said.
There you are then, David Kellner said...
well, my mum says you should come to the synagogue
and do Hebrew Classes.

So I went home and said,
Er David Kellner says I should go to synagogue
and do Hebrew Classes.
I see, mum said.

Hebrew classes were run by Mrs Kellner
but there wasn't a synagogue yet.
It was a corrugated iron methodist chapel
without any methodists in it.
Zeyde thought it was hysterical:
So Michael's going to *kheder*! Michael's going to *kheder*!
Zeyde didn't go to *shul* either,
he went to Hackney Downs instead
and stood around with a lot of old men in dark suits
with shiny bits on the *tukhes* of their *gatkes*.

At Hebrew classes Mrs Kellner who was very small
and had a huge and very wonderful bosom,
taught me the letters.
I could only remember two of them.
They both looked like the letter seven
but they each had a dot in a different place.
One of them had the dot over the top
and the other one had the dot in the middle.
How do you tell the difference, said Mrs Kellner?
I'll tell you.
(I never told David Kellner
that I loved his mother's wonderful bosom.)
What happens, she said
when you get hit by a football over your head?
You say OH!
And what happens
if you get hit by a football in your belly,
you say OOOH!
There you are
that's how you tell the difference.
One says OH!
And the other says OOOH!

This, I remember
but I left Hebrew classes
after they shouted at me on the outing to Chessington Zoo.
You don't have to learn Hebrew
from people who give you *tsurres* at Chessington Zoo.

New School

When I went to the new school
people noticed I was a Jew.

I was the only one.

So they did the jokes:
you know,

throwing a penny on the floor
to see if I'd pick it up

rubbing their noses

going 'my boy' and 'my life'
while they were talking to me.

And if ever I had to borrow any money
there'd be uproar
cheering, jeering,
'Don't lend him any money, you'll never get it back.'

Sometimes I'd go along with it
and I'd put on what I thought was
a Jewish voice
and say things like
'Nice bit of *shmatte*.'

It's like I was bringing *Zeyde*
into the playground
running round him going,
'You're a Jew. You're a Jew.'

It's like I was saying,
'Yes I'm a Jew
but I'm not like other Jews,
I'm an OK-Jew.'

268

But I wasn't.
For them I was just
Jew.

I was the Jew that it was
OK-to-say-all-the-foul-things-
you-want-to-say-about-Jews-to.

And I played along with it,
I thought it'd stop them hating me
but all it did
was make it easier for them
to hate all Jews.

School Visit 2

The name tag on her pinny says, Patricia Kaufpisch.
I'm going to ask her if she knows what it means...
her father must have told her...
no, her father didn't tell her...
no, I can't tell her in front of her friends...
I've got to say why they called her Kaufpisch...
maybe I will tell her that old German joke...

There were these Jews, right?
living in Germany about 200 years ago, right?
and they were called ben This and ben That
so these Germans said to the Jews
if you want to be citizens of Germany
you've got to have German names, right?
but it'll cost you...
and if you haven't got much money
(money, Jews, geddit?)
you'll have to buy ones like
Ochsenschwanz, Eselkopf, Saumagen and Hinkedigger:
Oxprick, Asshead, Pigbelly and Cripple.
So this Jew comes up to the German in charge of names
and he says, I've come to buy a name for myself
have you got any of those pretty ones?
Rosenthal, Valley of the Roses, that sort of thing?
Sure, says the man in charge,
but Valley of the Roses doesn't come cheap
what sort of money are we talking about here?
Oh I've hardly got two coins to rub together,
says the Jew.
So what do you do for living, son?
says the man in charge of names.
I sell things, a bit of this, a bit of that.
Fair enough, says the man in charge, fair enough.
How's this for size? Kaufpisch. Sellpiss.
...if I could talk to her on her own, I could tell her
but she's saying, goodbye, thank you for talking to us,

270

Mr Rosen.
Rosen? It means roses.
So?
I was one of the lucky ones.

English Literature

George Macbeth, poet, now deceased
told his school readers
that T.S. Eliot's 'apparent antisemitism'
was not 'significant' or 'dishonourable'
as such references were 'frequent and casual'
in the writing of the time.

So, dear students,
do not concern yourselves with this matter,
the antisemitism of any writer
in the first half of the twentieth century
is here certified normal.

What fun it is to be a critic
reading poems that are antisemitic
Eliot, Chesterton, Thackeray too
loved to write of the hateful Jew
and good old Gilbert of Sullivan fame
pitched in against the hateful same.
Cuddly Stevie Smith as well
wanted us to go to hell.
Our lives are so much the richer
for reading English Literature.

Burglary

I got burgled
they emptied out boxes
ripped open files
took the answer machine
and four harmonicas
not much else
oh yeah
three tapes I made
one was called
Hairy Tales and Nursery Crimes
one was called
Quick Let's Get Out of Here
and one was called
You Can't Catch Me
I suppose burglars have jokes
and I almost laughed...
after all they hadn't stolen much
and they hadn't broken anything...
but then I caught sight of something.
It was the only thing they broke:
they had smashed the glass of
a mounted photo of 18 *hassidim*
in their fur hats and white leggings
standing in Stamford Hill
carrying banners saying:

WE ARE ANTI-ZIONIST BECAUSE WE ARE JEWS

THE JEWS HAVE ALWAYS BEEN KNOWN AS
MERCIFUL

WE REQUEST THAT THE NAME ISRAEL
WHICH BELONGS TO THE JEWISH PEOPLE
MUST BE WITHDRAWN FROM THE ZIONIST STATE

ANTI-ZIONIST IS NOT ANTI-SEMITIC

IF ALL THE ARAB STATES RECOGNISE THE
ZIONIST STATE
WE WOULD STILL OPPOSE IT

It's best not to figure out
exactly what kind of person would want to
steal an answer machine, four harmonicas
three tapes for children with absurdly relevant titles
and also want to
smash a photo like that.

My Mother at the Undertakers

She was dead
it was before the funeral
when my father said he wanted to go and see her
did I want to come?

She was laid out in the backroom
strangely high
as if on a lab bench
with a sheet up to her chin

my father went in ahead of me
and stood next to her head
I wondered if we were doing this
because we were Jews

her skin shone like an insect
and her nose had shrunk down to a beak
this is all that's left
this is all that's left

I turned away but saw my father
lean in close to her
raise his hands into the space between his face
and hers.
For one moment I thought he was going to clap.
Then it seemed like he was going to hold her head.
Or perhaps his.
But what he did was shake his hands,
shake them in that space between his face
and hers.

It seemed like some ancient gesture
some blessing. Or curse. Or both.
Wishing her a safe passage?
Or cursing her for leaving him.
He stared and muttered
looked away and looked again.
I could see what he was doing:
forcing this picture into his mind,
making himself hold on to this last view of her
after forty years of knowing it like the back of his hand.
Or hers.

Nativity: now and then

The crib's lit. Shepherds stare.
Out-of-scale straw waits for impossible cattle-turds.
Mary looks like the woman from the Vidal Sassoon ad
Joseph, like me.

I remember this stuff.
I lived next door to St. Lukes
and December hometimes were delayed
when we lingered in the light of it.
Odd that we thought these unmoving plaster dummies
brought the story to life.

We? No.
I knew this wasn't my stuff.
It was theirs.
This Family didn't belong to me.
And even if the wiseguys were foreigners
Mary and Joseph were English, suburban,
from just up the road, had a sitting room
where you weren't allowed to play on Sundays,
spoke like my headteacher.

I envied my friends' treat
their way of warming themselves by the scene
but I didn't know then that she was a Miriam
and he a Yossef.

Jon Silkin

Death of a Son

(who died in a mental hospital aged one)

Something has ceased to come along with me.
Something like a person: something very like one.
    And there was no nobility in it
      Or anything like that.

Something was there like a one year
Old house, dumb as stone. While the near buildings
    Sang like birds and laughed
      Understanding the pact

They were to have with silence. But he
Neither sang nor laughed. He did not bless silence
    Like bread, with words.
      He did not forsake silence.

But rather, like a house in mourning
Kept the eye turned in to watch the silence while
    The other houses like birds
      Sang around him.

And the breathing silence neither
Moved nor was still.

I have seen stones: I have seen brick
But this house was made up of neither bricks nor stone
    But a house of flesh and blood
      With flesh of stone

And bricks for blood. A house
Of stones and blood in breathing silence with the other
    Birds singing crazy on its chimneys.
        But this was silence,

This was something else, this was
Hearing and speaking though he was a house drawn
    Into silence, this was
        Something religious in his silence,

Something shining in his quiet,
This was different this was altogether something else:
    Though he never spoke, this
        Was something to do with death.

And then slowly the eye stopped looking
Inward. The silence rose and became still.
The look turned to the outer place and stopped,
   With the birds still shrilling around him.
      And as if he could speak

He turned over on his side with his one year
Red as a wound
He turned over as if he could be sorry for this
And out of his eyes two great tears rolled, like stones,
       and he died.

The Coldness*

Where the printing-works buttress a church
And the northern river like moss
Robes herself slowly through
The cold township of York,
More slowly than usual
For a cold northern river,
You see the citizens
Indulging stately pleasures,
Like swans. But they seem cold.
Why have they been so punished;
In what do their sins consist now?
An assertion persistent
As a gross tumour, and the sense
Of such growth haunting
The flesh of York
Is that there has been
No synagogue since eleven ninety
When eight hundred Jews
Took each other's lives
To escape christian death
By christian hand; and the last
Took his own. The event
Has the frigid persistence of a growth
In the flesh. It is a fact
No other fact can be added to
Save that it was Easter, the time
When the dead christian God
Rose again. It is in this,
Perhaps, they are haunted; for the cold
Blood of victims is colder,
More staining, more corrosive
On the soul, than the blood of martyrs.

What consciousness is there of the cold
Heart, with its spaces?
For nothing penetrates
More than admitted absence.
The heart in warmth, even, cannot
Close its gaps. Absence of Jews
Through hatred, or indifference,
A gap they slip through, a conscience
That corrodes more deeply since it is
Forgotten – this deadens York.
Where are the stone-masons, the builders
Skilled in glass, strong first in wood;
Taut, flaxen plumbers with lengths of pipe,
Steel rules coiled in their palms;
The printers; canopy-makers –
Makers in the institution of marriage?
Their absence is endless, a socket
Where the jaw is protected neither
Through its tolerance for tooth,
Nor for blood. Either there is pain or no pain.
If they could feel; were there one
Among them with this kind
Of sensitivity that
Could touch the dignity,
Masonry of the cold
Northern face that falls
As you touch it, there might
Be some moving to
A northern expurgation.
All Europe is touched
With some of frigid York,
As York is now by Europe.

*This is the first part of a two-poem sequence, Astringencies.

One Image of Continuing Trouble

A Prayer Cup

As if steel, but a silvery
tar creeps upon Isaac
in Abraham's hand. Our Bible

is clasped in darkness. And for wine
three inches of the blood
of six million. The cup

wells Hebrew, and my grandparents
have tracked their kind into
the lake over-flowing

our curious feet. I who write
a factious poem want the means
to bless a christian. Breath

from the two locomotives *Work*
and *Freedom* steams over
the numbered faces.

Arbeit macht frei ('Work makes freedom')
mottoed the camp gates.

The Plum-tree

Our grave spittle covers his face.
Afraid I insult my God
of my poems I'll say little.

We married in late winter.
Mild as a pear, whose succulence
lured its priest. Yes, I said,
I believe; and miracles
balanced on pumiced hands. My door
glided shut.

I speak of the six million
and do not shave; no iso-rhythmic
evennesses of mind temper
the blithe compliant ratchets of industry;
and for the earth I work off, I earn
how much? We consider, and feed
the excellence of three cats.
When the sun undoes its pure,
fierce hands, I talk with the plum-tree
in the dene where mild limestone
kneels to the ice-floe. The tree's
incipience of fruit makes plump
the maidenly flowers: to what is torn,
wrenched, shot, or beaten, it can bring
nothing.
The dene's light crumbles. Of no use
if beauty affirm the techniques
work anneals; and, what droops away
is beauty as consolation – in the flame
work is of cash drudged for.
Barren are the plum-tree's flowers
fleshed as they glisten.

The Jews in England

I had no voice, and borrowing one I made English harsh,
which is your tender complex English.
It is your language, and I must look for mine.

Hear my speech, love, take notice, and stay within
    my acts.
I am your tender gentile woman, and you, Jew, have
    brought us this,
a poem that is a single note, of praise, the psalms
fresh as a changing glance, a fragrant look,
in an English we had not, but on our tongues
makes our lives new. Yet now, she is she, this tongue,
who will not come again, although I sit in grasses,
their flowering, their mutual forgiving allowance
of space, like feathery cats at a dish – the prairie,
with its miles of sound, which adjusted to each new comer,
until it has been cast up by the spade, its mattocked web.

I have no notion of how I shall die. I saw it die.
I see it, my brain, nails, digestion, all to decay into new
    earth.
Revolving its cutting edge, a thresher,
where wheat, stalk, haulm, and staff of floury seeds
like torches, stand, each eye broaching the same vision.
We face our God. And eat.

Tenderness

Not trusted with a key, I jar the front-door's lock,
its nice prevention held in my parents' hands.
A woman in the hall points flowers, scent and tungsten
showing grime in the tiles, their earth-hued triangles
of trunk, of bough, fruit and blossom making a tree.
The house is my parents' sanctuary,
therein
the woman, our hall's solicitous familiar,
like an oyster-catcher jabbering
a red bill for her endangered young.

My parents form a pearl
fit to pass through a space, to hold the staying loop
for blouse and shirt. May I touch you both?
We cannot touch. We speak of ships scudding to Palestine,
male Jews and passionate rigid women hoping
we will connect. We have wasted
our lives, waiting for tenderness.

My parents, my lovers, pour the tea
and let the swollen belly of pewter cool. The shop will
    stay open,
like a bulging lamp,
a topaz ossuary, its jovial thick-set beams
fuelled by the dead. The light feels barbaric,
this quiet rape of darkness,
a moth's wings clapping itself into life
that burns up right away.

Father, mother, your moth-like lives are never spent,
waiting for tenderness,
the nape of the neck will be kissed.

Jew

Wine's tempo lingers in a glass triangle
where a bulb distributes light through alabaster
on the wooden bar
pacific-thicketed, squirrel-red, sweat
greases. But each day steps in
a diligent cleaning-girl.
Brass knuckles hinge the counter-flap.
Creatures in wine jars mouth 'I want to die'
whose owner loves me. I must not say... but his skull's

heat –

'nothing more, thanks.' Stay
in your bottles, you gentiles.

Vengeful Vasco da Gama suffered
resistless mermaids, ineffable sea-flowers
their mating-gentle eyes locking with his
in this mossy shifting consistent sea-paradise,
freighting images home that he might cease from

licensed voyage.

God's aquarium, stare into the hole.
Things feather
like oar-blades across water, light
flips over this sordid little bar.
Desire is so strange. Fool.
I wait to feather the Christian woman who stares
at my concealed treasuries, finger-tips on the bar,
her stillness at my restless core. Jew. Foolish Jew.

Great Goddess rub your light all over me
that I may sail her
in God's breath; say *ruach*, say 'Jew' –
but all the time I am crying, 'Ruth, Ruth,'
gently, achingly,
Jew's name. Alien and close.
Her eyelashes, like rhythm
in God's hunger.

Endomorphic

This has to be sorted through.
You can't tell me anything about love
who said I am to be comforted.

I saw you ended, with isolated white flesh;
the mouth pursed, seemed to be complaining
bitterly of something. Had you pain? The nurse
nearly wept, 'you come three hundred miles late.'
Your white body unbreathing, you have conquered.

Your mouth had minced words, they were like scat,
you were tired, were on *schpilkers*, grinned
with intent knowing eyes raised upwards.
'Drink,' you asked for; your hands
tepidly clutched mine round a hot cup.
Any fluid did. Then you cat-napped. I mourn.
Dare I need you – the last papery intimation
of protection taken off. Mother, this love
has crept down the bore, the substratum,
and denies the velleity, which claims tenderness.
Teach me how to have loved you,
my ancient dear.

I am not weeping. I make this complaint.
Of our first child, 'he should never have been born.' So you
spoke,
denigrated our produce, with my first her.
He dropped a tear, died, this almond-headed child,
his clearness in the kitchen of enamel bowls keeping watch.
Nothing can gladden anything here.
I can't focus you, mother.
I put my shoulder to the car door
and shut the husk,
I, genuine unmourning article.

They knifed my silk, my only silk
shirt, that my lady had bought, little
yiddisher knife, insisting on death-grief
in the Hebrew way, me,
your blood relative, son & co. But at this time
I love sex, pure uninfant joy, her
who receives me. No interminglings,
mother. I feel the irritable plucking,
and scald of the cry, 'child child'.

At the grave, she and I touched your box
before you lowered in. I shovelled morsels
of earth, as I had done on others,
which these three young Jews, earth-spading
Jews, now put upon you – the uncuppable
bread of this earth, soil, thuds
of it. Space taken into itself.
They can say what they like;
the death certifiers did not authorize
your leaving, all they can say is, 'yes, it's true' –
your unscheduled ceasing; the collar-bone
of a hare is no more delicate
than my sentiment for this her.

Mother it is time to be lyrical.
There was a saviour,
and such was his unaggressing nature
the constitution of the kingdom was set up to accept all.
Don't even think it. No king ever was,
only the idea, his grief over each parted soul.
Don't be afraid, don't even
be angry. Go where the feasting tables are,
and decay, courageous then as thou wast here.
Shall we converse again? The clock runs on.
The archipelago, wet from tenderness
itself like spume blown. Permanently.

First it was Singing

From the first cry
I was given music with which to speak,
  Tramping the agape streets
      The amazed faces

Turning, with their
Voices to laugh at the singer in the common
  Street. From the first I was
      Given a voice

To cry out with.
It was a peaceable music tuned in fear.
  Later, it was death
      But it was singing

First.
And from that it was I loved the hopping birds,
  The limping fly
      And the mad

Bee, stung to anger
In worship of summer. It was their speech, and my speech,
  The Jewish stone and the
      Animal rock

Rolling together that made me sing
Of our common lash, the white raised weal across
  Our black back, I and
      The hunted fox, the

Huge fly, his
Dangerous wings torn from his body
  The seal tusking the sea,
      As the dog bawls air.

It was our harm
Made me sing. Afterwards it was death,
   Death of the stone
      By stoning

   The animal
By animals, but, first, singing.
   Jew and animal singing first;
      And afterwards, death.

Milkmaids

*(Lady's Smock)**

Ridging the stalk's length,
The pith ducts. You'd think
The leaves found by water. Their openness
Guards them; a giddy, a careless
Effusion of stem. That is strength.
From the topmost, a flower triumphs.
From each undomestic
Flare, four petals; thrown wide; a flexible
Unplanned exuberance.
A veined fat is under
The svelte integument;
A kind of vegetative warmth.
From the centre, axial, determined
Extend the stamens, long by usage
For survival, and grouped
Round the curt stigma. Nothing less enslaved,
Less domestic to man, they are twice free.
Will wander through your plot in whole families.
You will not cut milkmaids down.

That tender, that wild, strength
Sucks the untrammelled consciousness up.
They mount the incline breathless
Pale violet. Their eyes wide,
They halt at the wire. This is the camp.
In silent shock a multitude of violet faces
Their aghast petals stiff, at the putrescence
Of the crowd wired up. This halts them:
The showing bone; the ridges of famine,
Protrusions, want, reduction.

292

Silent also, they confront with their modesty
Of demeanour – the stiff fatigue
Of the sack jackets something altogether different
From those who supervise
In their soft, rigid cloth –
The prisoners confront
The unservanted faces of the plants.

Between their silences, comprehension; like the wire
Halted, staked, live.
Crowding through the tented cloth
That locust death, to each person.
For the flowers, the forked,
Upright sense of human
Creatures wanting patience, pulped, compounded into
    their children.

This poem is from the sequence, Flower Poems.

Jaffa, and Other Places

Toward Jaffa, foot-dragged sand is flattened, and pathed,
                                        the hardened grains
fusing then to a road, on which the fallen foot stifles.
                                Houses shake into dereliction.
A flat incohering of sand with bricks, remaining feet above,
                                                        stays.
A gulley cuts through these levels down, sprains in its
                                                sides, between
which pours brick, charred wood, tarpaulin, stopped.
                                                Inertia heaps:
mound of boots, motionless and brown, remains of the
                        mandate army, dispersed in England now.
Done with in worse places: shoes, crutches, irons, many
oddments, each similar, the inert teeth, ash, hair, dust
winnowed between grains of soil or not winnowed
                                                between them;
most of each category useful, separated. The flesh gets
                                        isolated from these,
the goods and its body harrowed apart. Each item heaps on
one of its kind, itself buried. Wardresses help sort each class.
And not the negro, his hunted skin finding each shadow
                                        not as dark as he
offers an absence as blank. Shortly the spider
is trained to bite at the organ; the bone round it liquifies,
                                                        the lips
of it attendant and limp. The Reich's swollen architecture
                                                will be less dank.
New immigrants near this ashy zone, pacified and burnt.

We Want to Survive

Sundown. The candelabra branches
seven flames. Sabbath is a taper.

The half-world douses sundown's fiery
indignant moral forms. Although

(surely) earth at its poles, flattened
like an orange, where blenched winds

precipitate with no end – earth tires;
inside that night we are its fires.

Is it against fire that one prays
each seventh day? Is every prayer

subliminal with earthly fear?
It's dark and the candles spit lightly.

Like hotel functionaries we hiss
with insulted life, who shrink with fire.

The cantor vomits wax, grease flares
his eminence. Six days' worldly fat

burn on the seventh's consuming thread;
is fire the meaning prayers endure?

Admit the mind through fire. Of no sex,
on the burnished silver flame assigns

as equal mild deliberate fire.
Look, Isaac; and do not touch.

Self makes its fire. Each outer flame
selves its next flame that bears a fire

gravid with inmost flame, no flame
that does not burn, is an unburning

inner moist wax light. I bring

my grandparents in an image in
inside the inmost flame. Old men,

someone's grandparents, though the sons
and their sons' sons are ash, someone,

some old man holding to the slack
rough skin of an old woman prodded

past child-bearing, some old men
are still grandparents. And they putter

their Hebrew as the cuffed wrist bares
and passes moist bread, that the hand

has blessed and split. Take it, Isaac,
since you know the language. The moth consumes,

and Hebrew prints the wings that sheet
in fire. An unburned darkish moist

prefiguring resumes the life
of memory that neither loves

nor does not, linked in dissolution
to what dissolves, but does not go.

Not just yet, Isaac; no, not yet.

Resting Place

In... c. 1230, John le Romeyn, then subdean of York
Minster, recorded the sale to the commune of the York
Jews of a plot of land in Barkergate adjacent to what was
already *antiquum cimiterium Iudeorum*. It is therefore on
that site, immediately west of the river Foss and now
under the tarmac of [a] civic car park, that archaeologists
will no doubt one day disturb the posthumous tranquillity
of Jews who can have rarely been completely tranquil
while alive.

The Jews of Medieval York and the Massacre of
March 1190 by R.B. Dobson, 1974, p.47.

1
   Where the camshaft weeps
oil, where the pained axle
   contracts

over Barkergate, what there is is still in pain.

The car, the cracked plated animal,
these oils weep by degrees back from their cells.

   Their crouched forms
tremble above our graves: Judah'd with oil
   their iron drips into our mouths.

What is it then, is it nothing?

   Earth's justice
cakes the skull with the clay's
   bronze confections,

                           we are
oil creeping to the Foss
where a sword rests its two edges:

297

it is not nothing to lie anywhere
   that they will let you. The sword
rusts like a child,

the Jewish child, the gentile sword; earth
   sells itself to us.

Camphored in oil, I lose all memory.

2

Church minds its force and men nurse souls but through
each passage, hope, a furled lamp casts its beam.

Of that Church, John; by whose furled lamp I sold
our loam for dormitory to the Jews.
Earth hold them gently, and be gentler to
this woman than her child is, nursing her
each part of death's submissions. To mind so
the flesh is nurse to death. If more life is,
then they must each become a door of selves
each enters by in suppliant need: their own.

They never heard of this. Angel of death
made of desire and mercy raise your wings.

Climbing to Jerusalem

(for Moshe and Ziona Dor)

The locomotive, a short
satisfied fierce horse, scores the plain
after which five carriages jangle.
At the mountain's jointing, with anemones
that spot blood, glimmering orange fruits
like memory tumble. A stuttering olive
pierces the terrace with age, being adored
as if a woman of a hundred.

The denser patches of anemone blood
the higher we thread – you abandon us.
We strew energy as Jerusalem
helmets its stone; the herdsman, His shadow
fractured with sheep.
Pure absence measures
the plain we leave –

its celestial wounding – where the stream moils
between trees slender as astonishment,
their long flanks
dressed with fingers. Amongst
glimmering wheels of fuel
the sacred catches fire with the world.

The Ship's Pasture

In the sun, the leaf, hesitant but active
this florescence of plain wood; with joy
I saw the fields of England, as new, chartered
shapes, bargained for, and so, snipped
with standing sheep, their snowy garments
by the limestone walls, bulbous fossils,
their thick inert forms braids dangling
the soft wealth of England: Selah. Except
some people here are brutal, the fist,
because of standing in the wrong place,
at the cheekbone. Fist, or snide
arrowy word.

I rose from England much refreshed, but returned
at evening; much undone that was once good
prior to this mean juncture. It was joy,
beside my self, to see the new fields. Whose
is this land that, like waiting flesh, turns
with a kiss, domestic, but yet is
a local habitation with no substance or name
sustaining it? It is the ship's pasture,
its interlinking husk of submarine,
sea-spike, the sleeted fields of destruction:
for payment, for emolument. I am
a part of this – the bee, cutter of wood,
whose timbered house is unimaginably
hospitable. This is what it is. Northwards,
a new Jerusalem with the lamb lies separate,
its shade dense and lovely. The woman
starts again, as though each portion of this
were knit afresh.

Jews without Arabs

Did we make them leave, did they turn the wheel
of dispersion? We flee
through desert prairie, those grasses
that never flower, though the cold at night
is the thought of the day's herbage
glimpsed in heat. Where are they, and the grasses?
They left, as if
we were boys to be shunned, without our sex,
miniature unicorns, but flatteringly;
like guano, like the bats' cave.
Their absence is our loneliness.
A fan full circle. If we stepped
into our shadow, we'd have no breath.

Here is a provision of bread the sun bakes,
a space in rock hiding Moses
God seeks to kill. We're Jewish Pharoahs
flicking water, whipping it. Canute's deathless stick
that parts the sea – fringed with Sinai's bog-cotton,
its flags of small dissension. All soldiers,
weapons, manuals, sweethearts
in kodak, sink, with the claws of a tank's tread
and the howling metal roar.
Ezekiel has bitter signs: in the lilac sky
his wheel turns
its inner circle in reverse. I free a soldier

like a fly, into desert meadows
of pebble, pale and fine as sugar. 'Unacceptable,'
in delicate abandon
in fine shunning wings, the mayfly cries.
She, the humming-bird's constant intrepid companion.
Theirs the mixed family of creation.
Our enemy's absence, which is the spear of loneliness,
an undying son we each have,
the unimaginable, unsought-for child
with us by a sandy spring, where we substantiate
our constant debarment – it mutely hammers
the dreaming part of our lives: a bruise, an inescapable
panic of inseparable pain.
The milk in our mouths is burnt for ever.
Friends, friends, what may we change to?

George Szirtes

Anthropomorphosis

Foreigners, said the lady. Off the bus
Fell two dark men in heavy duty jackets.
The conductor swore; a pair of dogs
Leapt after a ball in gusts of fretful barking.
The men stood at the kerb watching the bus
Disappear over the crest of the hill, then turned
Sharply and walked off in the opposite direction
Pausing only for one to let fly with a gob
Of spit toward the curving wall behind them.

It was as if I'd seen it all before –
That long sail of spit arching over.
By my will I held it there, suspended
Between brick and mouth. Slowly some
Indefinite memory broke, spilling its garbage:
A harbour town smelling of dead fish,
The uncertainty of leaving mingled with
Excitement at arrival. Years of water
Concentrated to a blob of spit
On its trajectory, and the afternoon
Rearranged itself around his act.

And though I could not say what place it was
Or how long ago, I too hung there
Encapsulated in that quick pearled light,
Spewed by his volition, about to crack,
The taste of sea already penetrating my mouth.

North Wembley

The mongol boy makes friends over the fence,
his cat owns all the local mice.
From hosepipes squirts the Sunday carwash.
Tom and Joan are decorating.

There are trees, grass verges, a parking space,
and alleyways, alleyways by the dozen.
Khan is arguing with his wife.
The train whistles through an empty station.
Blackberries by the railway are quickly stripped.
Jewish boys practise the violin in dark but modern lounges.

Over the main road there is a Sporting Club
with pitches stretching out to distant hedges
from where, one summer night, a lazy rat
emerged and crossed, legally, over the zebra.

Half Light

She is standing in a darkness that is luminous,
I say, but my cat flicks her green eyes upward
as if to reply, That is a lie, darkness cannot
be luminous unless I choose to make it so,
and she who is standing there inhabits darkness.
That argument is appropriate: I no longer know
who that woman might be. A dark croon of traffic
sings in my ears, plaster and brick
are four-square, both physical and mental space.
Yet someone is standing, waiting quietly
making that darkness luminous. I riffle
through my acquaintance, dead or living. A mother
dead too early burned brightly enough it is true
but would scarcely deign to blow to such thin flame
that darkness itself was the more noticeable –
Whose fingers if not hers then scratch away
behind the lids, causing the sensation of light?

The Green Mare's Advice to the Cows

i.m. Marc Chagall d.1985

'It seemed that the cow was conducting world politics at that time' – Marc Chagall

1

What matters is the price of the mare.
What matters is the colour of the street.
What matters is that streets have no colour to speak of
Until we give them colours. The same with names.
What matters is the sound of arguments
And not their content. Arguments are blue,
Which, incidentally, is the colour of the street
(And hence, you see, I show them arguing).
What matters is the Love of God
And never mind if God does not exist.
You make him yellow, just as Christ is white,
But that damn cockerel keeps getting in,
And cows with their seductive eyes and udders,
And violinists who can only scrape.
It is another music altogether
That we dance to – and it isn't much
But it will do, believe me, it will do.

2

Surrender to mere *brio*? Stiff
Heads float off in disbelief
And fingers multiply in grief.

A clock strikes midnight in the air
In homage to Apollinaire.
Let Malevich adore the square.

Those who are less innocent
Castrate, carve up, dissect, invent
With a much sharper instrument.

A brush is fine. In mute arrest
A country bumpkin cups the breast
Of tender Vacha. Cows are best.

Cows will run the government.
Cows have a delightful scent.
Cows produce their Testament.

You watch the carnival proceed
Down muddy streets. The cows will lead
The moujiks home while altars bleed

With gentle bovine sacrifice,
Both melancholy and precise.
You cannot kill the same cow twice.

You see the calf, you see the child
Within the womb: Vitebsk, a wild
Impatience, dirty, undefiled.

The commissars may rave and row,
The housepainters obey you now
And hang the banner of the Cow.

The frozen cow hangs like a star,
And you yourself a commissar –
You start to moo. Yes, you'll go far.

Remember Grandfather, who stood
Before you with his feet in blood:
'Now look here, cow, we must have food.'

First grub, then dreams. But Lenin stands
All topsy-turvy on his hands.
What sacrifice the state demands.

The cows will take you at your word,
Advancing on you in a herd.
One cow takes wing, soars like a bird.

But look up there. The dream clouds fly
Above nightmare artillery
And cows are raining from the sky,

Dead cows, contented cows. It pays
To trust their unaffected ways
And leave their ghosts a land to graze.

3

The Man who is a Cello and the Fish who plays
The Violin are suddenly struck dumb.
The Goat in the Sky grows horns of logic. He weighs
Too much and every puzzle and conundrum
Begins to feel the lack of a solution.
The puritans claim back their revolution.

The poet, no longer cut in pieces, does not lie
Flat on the grass in the formal posture of death.
The egotistic lovers neither kiss nor fly.
The riddled milkmaid sinks down out of breath.
The dead man's candles cannot light the street
And broken bodies rest on tired feet.

The village processions reverse their steps. They realise
The city they inhabit has always been there, waiting.
The samovar slips off the crooked table. The eyes
Of the dead calf are finally shut. The dating
Couples are dated. The pendulum is still
And time runs down like water from the hill.

4

Returning to the green mare. She is grinning
At the wild commotion. All those words and colours
Merely confirm her own view of aesthetics:
No artist ever paints quite what he sees.
No artist ever tries to paint his dreams.
An artist only paints what he believes in.
And she is winking, full of self-belief
And green intestines, though she knows the town
Is changing irredeemably behind her.
She tells the cows: your freedom is exciting.
She tells the cows: prepare for government.

The Child I Never Was

The child I never was could show you bones
that are pure England. All his metaphors
are drawn from water. His ears admit the sea
even to locked rooms with massive doors.

Look, let me make him for you: comb his hair
with venus comb, a wicked drupe for mouth,
twin abalones for ears, sharp auger teeth,
an open scalloped lung, a nautilus
for codpiece, cowrie knuckles, nacreous.
Let him shiver for you in the air.

The English schoolboy cannot understand
a country that is set in seas of land.

The child I never was makes poetry
of memories of landscape haunted by sea.
He stands in an attic and shows you his collection
of huge shells, and with an air of introspection
cracks his knuckle bones.

The Little Time Machine*

Burnt offerings: a little bonfire shivers
At the far end of the street, all rags and card
And insignificance. A wheelbarrow
Is propped like an old man kissing the pavement,
A stiff frock coat, the mud on the wheel his beard.
The flames leap and fall in rapid rivers
Of light, a confusion of elements.
I see small fires along the narrow
Passages between main thoroughfares.
The heart, the eyes and passions maintain
Their vigilance. The holocaust goes up
In smoke. Somewhere a soldier prepares
To set fire to fine details on a street map.

The map is always burning. Its consumption
Is conspicuous enough, imagined cities
Of fugitive colour, changing light on tiles,
Faces at windows, hands at doorways, feet
On trams and buses, clothes in smelly piles
In empty hallways, the sonorities
Of gossip and greeting. My friends and I meet
At restaurants, complaining of hard times
In the benevolence of an August night
That smiles on our children. We are an exception
To the rules of sleep. Our children will sleep light.
After the fireworks we tell old jokes
And pay our debt to history with rhymes.

The city dreams an island. It has always
Been here, stacked on its mound of days
Lapped by cold sea, pickled and saline,
Wearing, breaking off. Hard water furs
The kettles, houses fall, rejig the shoreline,
Everything is continually in friction
With the wind off the sea. The women with scarves,
The men pottering in sheds, seek protection
In distance, the insularity of it all.
Sad, great, shaggy country. The soldier hears,
Takes aim and fires but misses. Foreign flotsam
Adheres to the feet of piers by decaying wharves.
The ferries shuttle. Waves crack on the wall.

The crack of a gate. Time opens backward to
A heap of pebbles suspiciously like bodies.
The wind whistles through trains whose nightmare crew
Of passengers have fallen quiet, stopped
Their grimacing and squealing and have dropped
Where they stood, dropped off to sleep at last
In broken postures, parodies
Of grace, recumbency and carelessness.
It is only by imagining the trains
That I can enter the gate, walk across the field,
And wait for the signals to announce the express
Europa. Its carriages are sealed,
The wheels go rattling over broken chains.

Too long rejected, we meet up in the street
Below a lamp post, yellowed as old papers.
What news? we ask each other. Our faces
Are the cut-out shapes of childhood, full of creases
And torn edges, smudged and circled
In soft chalks. We've brought along with us
Giraffes and elephants in a discreet
Procession, with dolls and packs of cards, and pieces
Of furniture arranged in packing cases,
Nothing but dust and detritus.
This is the news, hot off the world's press.
It's late at night, you say. We are light sleepers,
I reply, our sleep is a kind of emptiness.

Somebody has escaped at last. Somebody gets married,
Has a child, another. Somebody remembers
Someone else or something, certain numbers,
Certain streets and faces. One is worried
By forgetfulness, another by clarity.
Someone is not sure they should be here.
    Down into the Metro, down the stair:
A drunken woman's weeping on a bench,
Another's sitting in a pool of water,
The humble familiar stench
Of loss. A fat policeman nudges
At them. The crowd skirts round the edges
Of the frame, spreads out into the city.

This sequence is from the longer sequence, Metro.

313

Flying Backwards*

The uncle with the chocolate factory,
The uncle who was magistrate,
The father who travelled to the States
And worked as a labourer. The middle class
Jews of Kolozsvár are the lost history
Of which she hardly spoke. Mother's bob
Is a fashionable frame for her neat face,
Which the edges of the photograph reframe.
They bind the sepia, prevent it spilling
Across the desk, hold names
At an aesthetic distance, where, by willing,
We can work them into fictions and animate
The past, which remains forever another place.

This poem is from a sequence of the same name, within **Metro**.

Grandfather in Green

My grandfather, the Budapest shoemaker
  wrote plays in his spare time, and then he died.
His body became a pebble on a beach
  of softness across which swept the pale green tide.

Pale green, I think, would suit him as a tint –
  under his eye, or thinly flexed across
the hooked bridge of his nose. His sour complexion
  was cooking apples, a summary of loss,

each a pucker in the flesh. His waistcoat
  was grey as clouds, a pale green handkerchief
blossoming from the pocket. Even his tongue
  would sit in his mouth, soft and green as a leaf.

And so he returned to nature after all,
  the pale green gall within him in the shut
cavern of his stomach, and the green
  smell of gas still lingering in the hut.

Losing

We lose each other everywhere:
the children in department stores
return as parents, *fils et père*
collide by the revolving doors.

The pavements' litter, burning flakes
of bonfires, tickets and franked stamps,
the fragile image drops and breaks,
the fugitive awakes, decamps.

The carriages uncouple, trucks
return unladen, suits appear
on vacant charitable racks,
the shelves of darkened stockrooms clear,

skin lifts and peels. A cake of soap.
The human lamps, the nails, the hair,
the scrapbooks' chronicles of hope
that lose each other everywhere.

Grandfather's Dog

His hat would sometimes precede him into the hall.
These were the bad days when everything went wrong
and the smell of leather followed him like a stray dog
across the carpet. It was a ghostly creature that slunk
about the flat, settling on chairs and cushions,
all soft retentive things would take him in,
the children, the women. The dog of course had suffered,
such was its nature, and such was theirs, the children and
women.

Because failure and humiliation are unexpected
the dog was to be expected. And sometimes it haunts me,
the thought of the dog. I've seen him sniffing
at my brother's ankles. His sheer size daunts me,
his dumb perseverance. I saw him once, sitting in the
kitchen
beside my mother, under her feet, at his most
persevering. He ate her slowly and left not a bone,
so I knew him to be a bitter and vengeful ghost.

And grandfather, the factory hand, was likewise eaten,
by him first, then gas, right from the beginning.
Even now as I walk through the town it is there, sharp
and pervasive, a smell of leather-tanning.

Soil

What colour would you call that now? That brown
which is not precisely the colour of excrement
or suede?
The depth has you hooked. Has it a scent
of its own, a peculiar adhesiveness? Is it weighed,
borne down

by its own weight? It creeps under your skin
like a landscape that's a mood, or a thought
in mid-birth,
and suddenly a dull music has begun. You're caught
by your heels in that grudging lyrical earth,
a violin

scraped and scratched, and there is nowhere to go
but home, which is nowhere to be found
and yet
is here, unlost, solid, the very ground
on which you stand but cannot visit
or know.

Rabbits

The rabbits are about their business
of softening. They congregate in gangs
by hedgerows as if waiting for an event
of greater softness to overtake them.
The clouds overhead grow rabbit scuts
and bolt across the field in evening dress.
The whole sky is purpling with the scent
of evening. A clock opens and shuts
time out. Flowers bend on a single stem
and wind plumps leaves to wings.

Rabbits flicker into open spaces
all by themselves, exploratory, vague,
bristling in the wind, apologetic.
Out of sight, they settle
delicately then hop away, their faces
dreamy and purposive. They are a thick-
ening in the dark, a curl of soft metal,
a wholly benevolent plague
for which woolly words have to be invented,
something earth- and dropping- scented.

They lollop about in silence for a while,
shiver and bob, consume, dart back
into their holes, peek out. Soon the field
swallows them whole. The clock claps
its hands. They run off scared. The wind
bursts from a hedge and over a stile.
Leaves mumble, their lips are sealed.
The train swoops down its sinister track,
and the clouds make dramatic shapes
in the sky which is dropping like a blind.

Something of terror remains in the grass
where the rabbits have been. Night
comes on as the negative of daylight. Where
is the bristling gone? Something is shaking the train.
An old man holds his cup in trembling fingers,
waiting for the tremor to pass.
Insignificant stations swim through the air
in a fog of names. Some warmth lingers
in them and hovers there like a stain,
or a bird or a figure caught in mid flight.

Jonathan Treitel

Cold Spell

A man is putting on a sweater in Jerusalem. Nothing has
                                    been completed yet:
the putting on is what he is in the process of.
The torso is encased whereas the arms
hang limp, not being the man's arms but the sweater's arms

as yet un-armatured about the man's arms.
For a moment anybody could think the man is minus his arms
when it is just a case of having mislaid them –
no flesh and blood inside the polyester

then one hand twisting itself back on itself forces itself
up into an armhole
and begins its quick-slow pull-push through
as does the other, un-idling, in turn.

Do not try this at home, boys and girls,
it will cause the sweater to stretch, even tear,
the above procedure is not in accordance with the
                                    manufacturer's recommendations
for *Sweater, putting on of the*

yet on balance perhaps superior
to the approved method requiring the simultaneous
broaching of headhole and armholes
 whereby there appears, temporarily, above the shoulders, a
                                    wobbly mass of contorted stuff.

A cold spell, now.
All across Jerusalem, men are putting on sweaters
or have put them on already – yes, consider these last first:
smart cosy folk.

You'd think there was nothing to it.
You'd think they'd never had to struggle.

The Great European Poem

Some kilometres ago I read the Great European Poem.
Misremembered quite where.
Daubed on a cave-wall?
Neither up nor down an Alpine pass, having clomped a good
                                        way on its elephant-feet?
Lost-and-not-yet-found in the Channel tunnel?
On a Viking funeral-pyre, all its stanzas ablaze, halfway
                                        up the Volga?
Syllables of it still twinkle at low tide.
Clinking fragments crawl to the surface, where they
                                        shouldn't be, by rights.
But there you have it.
Even its language is neither here nor there. "Do you speak
                                        Europeanish?"
They say it retreated from Moscow with snow on its
                                        line-breaks.
An after-rhyme twitched a dew-web in a copse in
                                        Pomerania.
Nothing left of it now, except an ache in a phantom verse,
and a stench of burning.

Tel Aviv Airport

1.

Where do men choose to create an airport?
Why, any not too rough terrain will do
reasonably adjacent to an urban concentration.
Then they come with special machines
to flatten the flatland flatter, and they lay on
the concrete runways and the duty free facilities
and the patient men who dream into
the luminous images of X-rayed luggage.

And if the town is by the sea – why then
they'll establish an airport by the sea:
the surf will spit at the retractable landing gear.
And if it's in the mountains – then they'll slap it on a plateau.
And if there's nowhere in the vicinity remotely suitable –
no flatness for hundreds of miles, the entire
rugged country a crisscross of angled slopes –
the airport will be built somewhere somehow.

2.

And in the Talmud there are many discussions along the lines of:
one man is the proprietor of a field of sesame whereas another
claims the right to an olive tree growing smack in the middle of it.
So who should have what, and when, and under which

arrangements
is debated by the rabbis at length by analogy to numerous other
arguably similar cases. And the rabbis have thoughts. And the

rabbis
have thoughts. And meanwhile the sesame ripens and is

harvested
and grows up into halva. And an olive is chewed by a man who

spits
the sucked stone out in the middle of a different man's field.

The Golem of Golders Green

I am searching in the attic of my family house.
Next to the dust, the rafters, the historic *Reader's Digests*,
the retired armchair with leaking upholstery, the roll upon roll
of wallpaper leftovers, the speaking doll that doesn't...
is a box stacked with my unused barmitzvah gifts: books,
mostly – and here's one that will do to begin with:
The New Standard Jewish Encyclopedia.
I thumb through its alphabetical order: discover –
jostled between Golgotha and Sam Goldwyn who said:
Begin with an earthquake and rise to a climax –
what I have been looking for.

The rusted catch on the leaded window jiggles;
undoes. My head protrudes
into London. There, to the right, I see –
were it not for the blocks of flats, the line-ups of semi-detacheds,
poplars, horse chestnuts, and the lie of the land –
clear to the artificial lake on Golders Hill Park.
Around it, an old woman in a wheelchair is pushed;
a Filipina servant jogs on her day off;
a Hassidic father crouches, lowering his earlocks
for his son to tug; a park keeper shouts a warning to
too-eager kids coming close to the brink
as they throw their bread on the water.
The ornamental birds lap it up. Ripples overlap like chain-link,
    and part
magic-trickily. I observe
irridiscent mallards, the superficial paradox
of black swans imported from New Zealand,
a hunger of ducks, an implausibility of flamingoes...
and, by the edge, on a patch of shining mud,
an old man with a book and a stick in 1573.

He is Rabbi Yehudah Loew, the Maharal of Prague.
Times are bad. The Inquisition sputters on. Sephardim are still
leaking away from Spain. News is coming through
of the troubles in Mainz, not to speak of
the events at Worms. Somebody stepped out
the other day onto Golders Green Road without glancing left
and was run over: I had been at school with him.
A friend of my parents has a growth in the rectum.
Rudolf II has an air of tolerance, but...
We need a messiah – or failing that
at least an odd-job-man to do the rough work.
A flaming brand
glimmers smokily on the banks of the Vltava
at midnight four centuries ago where the Maharal,
high on fasting and chanted penances,
scratches with his stick on a silted shore. He sings
Genesis 2:7 – God breathes
into Adam's nostrils. He sketches
the shape of a man. He paces around it,
clockwise, seven times. He scrolls his manuscript of
the Book of Formation.
He reads
an alphabetic acrostic which I,
with my torso in an attic and my head
in open air, and you,
moving your finger down this page,
are reading:

Arra
B'ore
Golem
Dovek
Hachomer
V'tigzor
Zeidim
Chaval
Torfei
Yisrael

(You create the Golem, made from mud,
to defeat the wicked, the ravagers of Israel)

The torch gutters out. The mud glows, sizzles,
swells into some-
thing or
body who
arises,
naked, male, soul-free – amazing
the Filipina, the Hassid, me, the park keeper, the wheelchair
woman
and the kids scattering crumbs.
The scared birds flap to the far end of the lake.

Let's dress this Golem, then,
in a skein of old legends. Give him the dark heart
of Mary Shelley's Frankenstein's monster. Lend him an
oblong suit
stripped from a flickering black-and-white Boris Karloff.
Equip him with the brute power of Karel Capek's Robot.
Assign him the mindless intelligence of Isaac Asimov's
UNIVAC.
Stamp a Name of God on his brow – *Emet* – Truth –
as in the Habimah Theatre's long-running blockbuster.
Or just kit him out with second-hand rags
(as the Maharal did): a holey cloak, too-big boots
slightly punctured; and beckon.

The Golem follows. His boots' iron tips,
ringing on the cobblestones, strike sparks.
A yellow star is pinned over where his heart's not.
He takes the path through the vegetable market and
the meat market
rising to the Ghetto in the shadow of the Castle. Or
he saunters
through Golders Hill flower garden. He admires
the brilliance of daffodils and the impertinence of snowdrops.
He lowers a stiff paw to stroke a crocus. He squeezes

327

a sprig of lavender: it gives up its perfume. He nods to an old tune
that an oompah band on the bandstand is banging out. Or he
                                        stands at the back
of the Altneu shul while the Maharal is intoning Kaddish.
The rabbi rests his palms on the creature's head.
"This is a mute I found by the river. Let him stay. I will care for
                                        him."
The Golem tells the time by the horloge on the Ghetto Town Hall
(its hours are marked in Hebrew; its hands move
                                        counterclockwise)
or the Cenotaph by the Golders Green bus station
(its face is fixed permanently at midnight).
He is assigned commandments:
sweep the rabbi's floor; guard the Ghetto gate;
drop into Grodzinski's for a kilo of Israeli couscous in a
                                        cellophane bag;
pick up the usual at the Bagel Bakery...
He pauses under where the sign was: Buy Bloom's Best Beef.
He scrapes the mud off his soles on the welcome mat of the
                                        Public Library,
finds himself under bars of fluorescent lighting. Past
General Fiction, Crime, Psychology, Selected New... and ends up
                                        in the corner,
kneeling beside Judaica. He is used to his dark niche
in the Maharal's study, brooding on nothing but his
                                        rabbi at the lectern
assembling Talmudic commentaries – wonderful
                                        pensive wrangles –
which I have the Golem pull from the stacks, along with stories
by the Brothers Singer and the Brothers Grimm,
by Poe and Shelley, by Ozick and Aleichem,
Winkler's (New York, 1980) monograph on the Golem mythus...
Hump them to the light-pen operated check-out... and up
to here and now in the attic.
Volumes multiply around me in towers and crenellated walls
like a Build Your Own New Jerusalem construction kit
not assembled according to instructions.
Bookmarks, trapped in the jaws of closed books, flutter.

Books flap open on deliberately creased pages. Flick and browse.
My pen squawks. My notes rustle. Variant legends congregate...
There is a good Jewish virgin: there is a wicked Christian priest.
There is a pig and a dead baby, *Pesach* and Easter,
a small corpse dumped in a ghetto yard, a charge of
ritual murder –
which the Maharal refutes by dint of superior wisdom
and his Golem's strength... And what of history?
No blood libel stuck in the age of Rudolf. So they all lived
happily ever...

Conduct a wordsearch under 'GOLEM' on a database of
rabbinical responsa.

1. Can a Golem speak?
2. May a Golem form part of a minyan for prayer?
3. Has a Golem a soul?
4. Will a Golem be resurrected at the end of time?
5. Can a Golem father a child?

1. Only living men can speak.
2. No – because he is not one of the Children of Israel.
   Yes – because he is an adopted orphan. Both
replies are given.
3. His soul is not like ours; but he has a spark of the divine –
and so
4. he will be resurrected.
5. Adam, moulded from earth, was a Golem before
he was a Man.

A Golem was the first father.

In the topmost storey of the Altneu shul,
the Maharal erased the aleph from the Golem's brow, making
Emet into *Met* – meaning Death.
The creature became mud and wormy dust again.
The Maharal slammed and locked and double-locked the door
                                                    after himself,
staggered to ground level,
and proclaimed
that never again should anyone ascend the turning staircase,
unlock the attic door, and disturb the Golem's remains.
And in every generation since, we have been climbing
the stairs and twisting the key in the lock.

Daniel Weissbort

The Name's Progress

At seven I was re-named Whitbord
by the headmaster of The Hall School, Hampstead.
It was 1942.
My actual surname, he explained,
was too German.

Weissbort, the name, was antipathetic.
Later, I surmised
it was a corruption of
Weissbart or Weissbrot –
these were no better.
For a while, though, I was Whitbord,
so very whinglish and whistleclean
that a continental, francophone mum-and-dad
scarcely disturbed my equanimity.

How did Mr Wathen light upon it?
My imagination falters. Perhaps, simply:
'We'll call him Whitbord.'
I doubt whether, properly speaking,
we were ever consulted...

All right, so he wasn't an anti-Semite,
at least not by the standards of those times...

Later, after the war,
Weissbort once again, I wondered why
my name had had to be changed.
But then, I often had to answer questions like:
Is that a German name?
No, in parentheses,
voiced or more usually unvoiced:
It's Jewish...

In England, they still occasionally ask,
in America never.
One reason to prefer America?

Fifty-nine

He didn't quite make it,
staggered once, twice,
and was down.

Destiny, it had to be,
stood in the way.
It lashed out, flailed.
There was no getting by.

So, he never crossed over
from what was all contention
to tranquillity and gazing on vistas.

He never moved past
the roomful of quarrels,
the barterings and negotiations,
the plethora of objects.

He never took the crucial step,
leaving all that behind,
becoming aware of what may be
when suddenly all is permitted,
the prohibitions lifted,
the threats and judgments suspended.

For him, there was no sequel.

So, his spirit,
its tragic muteness,
has remained with me,
his sacrifice has ended at my feet.

He was consumed by age fifty-nine,
striving mightily to the very last.

My Country

My country?
What is my country?
It never spoke to me,
assuming all was well.

But all was not well.
I didn't know,
didn't and still don't,
though I wait,
hopeful as ever.

In England I was born.
Anticipation was my lot.

Yom Kippur at the British Museum

Entering the courtyard, I gasped,
seeing a Jew bowler-hatting happily to "shul,"
clasping his prayer-book proudly,
and remembered suddenly –
my wife had thrown it in my way at breakfast ...
breakfast! –
"It's Yom Kippur."

And climbing the steps, my first impulse –
what if I fast three days instead of one,
read the whole prayer-book through,
or go to "shul" on Saturdays –
sickens me. Ach!

And as I sit down it begins.
Enviously I remember that "day off,"
that different day,
when I actually came to love my fellow Jews,
and in general a high point for the year to run up to
and away from.
I sit, hatless and cold,
where today I notice many empty seats,
among students of chess, Portuguese literature,
nuclear strategy, racing horses.
Can I call myself one of the Jews
that I should choose to be in this madhouse,
rather than in that,
on this Day of Days?

But what is the Day of Atonement particularly?
Think! Answer!
It is a day which, by itself, might sustain Jewry,
it is a day encompassing a year,
a day of accounts,
of speculation, resignation, acceptance finally,
a day hot with griefs, joys, fears, hopes,
a day demanding much of an ordinary Jew,
which he could not endure unshared.
How can I, seated under the dome,
hope to make this effort on my own?

Nervous as a solitary hen
my writing flutters on and on.

The trouble is –
while I would not return to the tyranny of the old lion,
I am no emancipated Jew,
nor liberal Jew even.
I am no rationalist, no agnostic.
Rejection of orthodoxy seems to me impertinent –
I cannot take refuge in claiming
that it is on my own account alone –
and now I am afraid to curse God, even in jest;
yet belief does not flower.

Folded over my desk I sit
at the entrance of the synagogue,
contemplating a prayer-shawl,
fingering a prayer-book.
I listen to the old chants in my mind.
Some take me maybe for a beggar.
Bad-tempered beadles beckon me inside.
What can I do except sit
and shake my head?

Memories of War

In this green and pleasant land,
where V1s and V2s
were not aimed specifically at Jews,
I played Nazis, Nasties
on the bombed sites.

We collected shit-coloured, sky-fallen metal.
My stomach still turns from the time
I picked up a bit of shit instead...

But why here and not
Lodz, Warsaw, Brussels, Paris?
I went on growing.
With nostalgia, I remember
"Onward Christian Soldiers" and
"To be a Pilgrim."

Father's Anniversary

August –
and it's hot, as on the day you were buried.
We walk stiffly up the long path,
identify the row, stop
before your double bed-sized slab.

Now, as each year, I try to think of you,
to form a prayer,
suppressing the faint impulse to shout.

She stoops. She places a pebble on your slab,
then raises her head:
she spells out the inscription on the stone,
as though confronted by it for the first time.
Doing duty for you who lie there,
she interprets the Hebrew letters.
We cough, murmur, and nod.
We do not look at one another –
there's this to look at.
Finally, she turns –
too soon for me, though nothing's to be gained by staying.
Heads bowed, we file back to the path,
leave you to yourself.

Returning to the car park,
absently – irreverently? – we read
the inscriptions carved on other stones.
Resigned yet at the same time shocked,
we note, as always,
how the dead have increased
since our last visit.

In the back seat,
she shuts her eyes.
She slumps, not so much overcome
as conserving herself.
In front, slowly,
we loosen our collars,
remove our skull caps,
roll down the windows.

So English

When I was a child, I knew kids like you,
I wanted to be like them,
to grow up like them,
not The Wandering Jew.
But evidently it takes two generations.

Later I emigrated to America.
Of course I'd no hope ever of arriving,
but I left you, my children,
and the me who was becoming just a bit like you,
so English.

From Aegina

Allow me to write you a line or two,
not a really long poem –
I leave that kind of thing to you –
and no metaphors with Greece in them, I promise ...

For I shall always recall your compassionate mockery,
and immediately following, ingenuously, the seriousness
of your deep sure-footed voice, used to negotiating crags,
that flawlessly,
with the confidence of accomplished oratory,
of ritual dance,
demonstrates the force and equilibrium
of the Man-God.
And your dark sober eyes too,
at the same time regarding me, I love and honour –
See, I am using words out of the marriage ceremony!
And your vulnerability,
your face that seems to turn upward,
as if waiting for someone's brutal palm to press it down;
that seems to say:
I can take it, and besides
I have no choice! –
your absolute vulnerability, constituting toughness,
because you have no choice,
and know it –

You explode at the foolhardiness of some new adventure,
some new jousting with the forces out to get you.
And how I shall miss your telling of this, so unaccountable...

Protest

"You see, I'm very fond of trees ..." said I
to the retired man who had been cutting down trees in his
yard,
and had just cut one down on the border with ours.
I tried to stop him, crying:
"Excuse me sir, excuse me sir!..."
But of course he couldn't hear over the scream of his
chainsaw.
Now he and his wife squatted on the slope of the gully,
listening to my futile remarks.
They gazed wide-eyed, in sympathetic understanding.
"So are we," he said, nodding vigorously,
and then explained that the trees were so close together
they didn't grow right, just tall –
"Like a pole," he said, pointing at the fallen tree –
and that he was going to plant new trees.
They too valued their privacy, wanted to be screened from our
house, as we did from theirs –
I shrugged politely.
"We're thinking of a willow," he said speculatively.
"It gives lots of shade and is fast growing."
Even disarmed as I was by their mildness, I wondered...
Fast? How fast? Five, ten, twenty years?...
Later it occurred to me, too, how anomalous a willow
    would be here,
where what grew naturally was a tangle of scrubby oak,
    box-elder, locust, and mulberry –
"Messy trees," his wife had called these last.
His expression and hers, full of solicitude,
was unchanged all the time we talked.
They heard me out, as you'd listen to someone who'd got
hold of
the wrong end of the stick,
who hadn't quite understood it was for the best,
but maybe was just beginning to,
and with a little patience...

They wanted all their trees to be full,
with plenty of light and air,
not crowded, intertwining, struggling for *lebensraum*.
They wanted all the death and dying to be dragged out into
the open and taken away...
This morning the tree was chopped up, piled neatly on the
sidewalk, like a funeral pyre, alongside the garbage cans.
And I remembered with a pang
that moment when his saw ended its life,
with me helplessly crying,
"Excuse me sir, excuse me sir!"

How Death Came About

1.
When God created life he created death too,
but seeing what a good time was being had by all,
he hadn't the heart to let it loose.
Instead he visited people with boils and sores,
with the plague which would have carried them off
                                         wholesale,
with domestic strife, which drove many to the brink,
until they cried out: Lord, Lord, relieve our suffering!
Whereupon God sent death to them,
in answer to their prayers.

2.
The man Adam said to his wife Emily,
My dear, since we agreed always to be honest with one
                                         another,
I have to tell you there's this woman Eve...
But Emily didn't let him finish.
She had been afraid of this from the start
and now she began to heap curses on Adam, Eve,
and above all on God, who had assigned her the role
   of eternal sufferer and victim,
abandoned wife and...
well, at least there weren't any kids.

Eve, cold-eyed, was meanwhile waiting in the wings,
wearing a sheath dress and nothing on underneath.
God regretted having started the whole business,
he couldn't stand the woman's tears.
For the first time he wished there were a higher authority
    he could refer the matter to.
Finally, he laid a mighty finger on Emily's trembling
                                      shoulder.
Child, he whispered earthshatteringly,
I admit I made a mistake.
To save you from further humiliation and suffering,
I shall take... No! shrieked Emily, but too late.
Eve sauntered into the room. Adam wept.

A Jew Watches You Fish*

I leaned against a rock
as you fished.
It was quite straightforward,
the line cast,
the fly drawn back across the current.

This seemed perfunctory to me.
Or had it been simplified, for my benefit?
I didn't think so, such was not your way –
just that the ritual was well-established.

Once, twice you nabbed a salmon,
said I brought you luck.
I told myself I was a kind of mascot –
a Jew and the fish with blood on its lips!

At this moment of strictly limited horizons,
of silenced protest,
I scurried as it were, between ghettos.

The way was windy, the flesh crawled in vain,
as I watched you cancel the living thing
with a blow to the brain.

*This is from a sequence of poems, Letters to Ted. David Weissbort and Ted Hughes co-founded Modern Poetry in Translation.

Contributors

Dannie Abse was born in Cardiff in 1923. After qualifying as a doctor, he worked as a specialist in charge of a chest clinic until 1982. His most recent book of poems, *Be Seated Thou,* was published in New York by The Sheep Meadow Press and his updated autobiography, *A Poet in the Family,* will be published in September 2001 by Pimlico. He is a Fellow of the Royal Society of Literature and President of the Welsh Academy of Letters.

Richard Burns was born in London in 1943. He has lived in Greece, Italy, the USA, and the former Yugoslavia. His poetry has been translated into ten languages. Burns has received several literary awards, including the Wingate-*Jewish Quarterly* Prize in 1992.

Ruth Fainlight was born in New York City in 1931, and has lived mostly in England since the age of fifteen. Her many books include poetry, short stories, translations, plays and opera libretti. Fainlight's poetry has been published in French, Portuguese and Spanish.

Elaine Feinstein was born in Lancashire in 1930. She is a poet, poetry translator, novelist and biographer of Pushkin, Marina Tsvetayeva and Bessie Smith. Her writings have been translated into twelve languages, including Hebrew. Feinstein's poems included here are from *Selected Poems*, apart from 'Amy Levy', 'Allegiance', 'Prayer' and 'Bonds' from *Daylight* and 'Prayer for my Son' from *Gold*, all published by Carcanet.

Karen Gershon was born in Bielefeld, Germany in 1923. She wrote several volumes of poetry, and edited *We Came as Children: A Collective Autobiography of the Kindertransport*. Her awards included the *Jewish Chronicle* book prize in 1967. Karen Gershon died in 1993.

Michael Hamburger was born in Berlin in 1924, has lived in England since 1933, and taught German at various universities till 1964. He was Visiting Professor in several American colleges, and has published major collections of translations from the German (Hölderlin, Celan, Rilke and Goethe), as well as drama and prose. He is the author of many volumes of poetry and of literary criticism.

Philip Hobsbaum was born in London in 1932. He founded the "Group" of poets at Cambridge in 1955, and edited *A Group Anthology* in 1963. Six volumes of Hobsbaum's verse appeared between 1964 and 1972. Since that time, he has concentrated on literary criticism and teaching at the University of Glasgow.

Michael Horovitz was born into a rabbinic family in Frankfurt in 1935, and brought to England at the age of two. He edits *New Departures* publications and organises its associated festivals (including *Poetry Olympics*) and recordings (including *Grandchildren of Albion Live*). Horovitz has published many volumes of poetry, as well as translations and anthologies, and is currently developing his visual art which includes "picture-poems" and jazz-inflected "paintry." Details available from New Departures, PO Box 9819, London W11 2GQ.

Arthur C. Jacobs was born in Glasgow in 1937. He lived, variously, in England, Israel, Scotland, Italy and Spain (where he died in 1994). Many of Jacobs' poems, unpublished or uncollected at his death, are gathered together with his published work in *A.C. Jacobs: Collected Poems & Selected Translations* (The Menard Press/ Hearing Eye, 1996).

Bernard Kops was born in London in 1926. His first book of poems appeared in 1955, and his latest, *Grandchildren and Other Poems*, in 2000. He has also published novels, autobiographies and many world-acclaimed plays.

Lotte Kramer was born in Mainz, Germany in 1923. She came to England, aged sixteen, as part of a *kindertransport*. Kramer has published several volumes, including *Selected and New Poems 1980-1997*.

Peter Lawson was born in London in 1960. He researches and teaches English and Jewish literature at the University of Southampton. Lawson's essays and reviews have appeared in *The Times Literary Supplement*, the *Jewish Chronicle* and *The Jewish Quarterly*. He is style editor of an Anglophone Israeli arts journal, *The Jerusalem Review*.

Joanne Limburg was born in London in 1970. She won an Eric Gregory Award for her poetry in 1998. Limburg's first volume, *Femenismo* (2000), was shortlisted for the Forward Prize for the Best First Collection of that year.

Emanuel Litvinoff was born in London in 1915. Among his many publications are novels, short stories, plays for stage and television, and four volumes of poetry. Litvinoff is editor of *The Penguin Book of Jewish Short Stories* (1979).

Gerda Mayer was born in Karlsbad, Czechoslovakia in 1927. She came to England, aged eleven, as part of a *kindertransport*. Mayer has written several volumes of verse, some of which are for children. Her latest collection is *Bernini's Cat: New & Selected Poems* (1999).

Jeremy Robson was born in Llandudno, Wales in 1939. He shot to fame as part of the performance poetry scene in London during the 1960s. For many years the *Tribune* poetry critic, he has published three volumes of poetry, recorded several LPs of his work for Argo, and edited a number of anthologies of contemporary poetry.

Michael Rosen was born in Harrow, Middlesex in 1946. He has published many books of fiction and poetry for children, and won several awards, including the Smarties' best children's book of the year award in 1990. His two volumes of poetry for adults are *You Are, Aren't You?* (1993) and *The Skin of Your Back* (1996), both available from Five Leaves.

Jon Silkin was born in London in 1930. From 1952 he was the editor of the literary journal *Stand*, originally in London, and from 1960 in Leeds and, later, Newcastle. He was a prolific critic and poet, publishing over twenty volumes of verse. Jon Silkin died in 1997.

George Szirtes was born in Budapest in 1948, and arrived in England as a refugee aged eight. His first volume, *The Slant Door* (1979), won the Geoffrey Faber Prize. Other prizes followed. To date, Szirtes has published a dozen volumes of verse, as well as translations of several Hungarian poets.

Jonathan Treitel was born in London in 1959. His poetry has been published in several journals, and appears in *Poetry Introduction 7* (1990), a Faber & Faber anthology of new poets in Britain. He is the author of two novels, *The Red Cabbage Café* (1990) and *Emma Smart* (1992).

Daniel Weissbort was born in London in 1935. He co-founded the journal *Modern Poetry in Translation* with Ted Hughes in 1965, and continues as editor. He spent nearly thirty years in America, at the University of Iowa, as Director of the Translation Workshop. Weissbort is the author of several volumes of poetry, and over a dozen translations of mainly Russian poets.

Select Bibliography

Abse, Dannie
Arcadia, One Mile (Hutchinson, 1998)
Selected Poems (Penguin, 1994)
Remembrance of Crimes Past (Hutchinson, 1990)
White Coat, Purple Coat: Collected Poems 1948-1988
    (Hutchinson, 1989)

Burns, Richard
The Manager (Bellew, 2001)
Against Perfection (The King of Hearts, 1999)
Black Light (The King of Hearts, 1995)
Learning to Talk (Enitharmon, 1980)

Fainlight, Ruth
Sugar-Paper Blue (Bloodaxe, 1997)
Selected Poems (Sinclair-Stevenson, 1995)
This Time of Year (Sinclair-Stevenson, 1993)

Feinstein, Elaine.
Gold (Carcanet, 2000)
Daylight (Carcanet, 1997)
Selected Poems (Carcanet, 1994)

Gershon, Karen
Collected Poems (Macmillan, 1990)

Hamburger, Michael
Intersections: Shorter Poems 1994-2000 (Anvil, 2000)
Collected Poems 1941-1994 (Anvil, 1995)
Selected Poems (Carcanet, 1988)

Hobsbaum, Philip
Women and Animals (Macmillan, 1972)
Coming Out Fighting (Macmillan, 1969)
In Retreat and Other Poems (Macmillan, 1966)
The Place's Fault (Macmillan, 1964)

Horovitz, Michael
A New Waste Land
  (New Departures, 2001)
Wordsounds & Sightlines: New & Selected Poems
  (Sinclair-Stevenson, 1994)
Growing Up: Selected Poems and Pictures 1951-79
  (Allison & Busby, 1979)

Jacobs, Arthur C
Collected Poems & Selected Translations
  (Menard Press/Hearing Eye, 1996)

Kops, Bernard
Grandchildren and Other Poems (Hearing Eye, 2000)
Barricades in West Hampstead (Hearing Eye, 1988)

Kramer, Lotte
The Phantom Lane (Rockingham Press, 2000)
Selected and New Poems 1980-1997
  (Rockingham Press, 1997)

Limburg, Joanne
Femenismo (Bloodaxe, 2000)

Litvinoff, Emanuel
Notes for a Survivor (Northern House, 1973)
A Crown for Cain (The Falcon Press, 1948)

Mayer, Gerda
Bernini's Cat: New & Selected Poems (Iron Press, 1999)
Monkey on the Analyst's Couch (Ceolfrith Press, 1980)

Robson, Jeremy
In Focus (Allison & Busby, 1970)
Poems Out of Israel (Turret, 1970)
Thirty Three Poems (Sidgwick and Jackson, 1964)

Rosen, Michael
The Skin of Your Back (Five Leaves, 1996)
You Are, Aren't You? (Mushroom Bookshop/Jewish
    Socialist Publications, 1993)

Silkin, Jon
Testament Without Breath (Cargo Press, 1998)
Selected Poems (Sinclair-Stevenson, 1994)
The Lens-Breakers (Sinclair-Stevenson, 1992)

Szirtes, George
The Budapest File (Bloodaxe, 2000)
Portrait of my Father in an English Landscape
    (Oxford University Press, 1998)
Selected Poems 1976-1996
    (Oxford University Press, 1996)

Jonathan Treitel
Poetry Introduction 7 (Faber & Faber, 1990)

Weissbort, Daniel
What Was All the Fuss About? (Anvil, 1998)
Neizsche's Attaché Case: New & Selected Poems
    (Carcanet, 1993)

Other Anthologies

*A Big Jewish Book: Poems & Other Visions of the Jews
from Tribal Times to Present*, edited by Jerome
Rothenberg, with Harris Lenowitz and Charles Doria
(Anchor Press/Doubleday, 1978)

*The Dybbuk of Delight: An Anthology of Jewish Women's
Poetry*, edited by Sonja Lyndon and Sylvia Paskin
(Five Leaves, 1995)

The Penguin Book of Hebrew Verse, edited by T. Carmi
(Penguin, 1981)

The Penguin Book of Modern Yiddish Verse, edited by
Irving Howe, Ruth R. Wisse, and Khone Shmeruk
(Viking Penguin, 1987)

Voices Within The Ark: The Modern Jewish Poets, edited
by Howard Schwartz and Anthony Rudolf
(Avon, 1980)